Ten Words
That Will Change
EVERYTHING
You Know About
GOD

Seeing God As He Really Is

Dr. Jim Richards
& Chaim Bentorah

Copyright © 2019 Dr. Jim Richards and Chaim Bentorah All rights reserved.

No part of this publication may be reproduced, stored, or transmitted in any form or by any means, including written, copied, or electronically, without prior written permission from the author or his agents. The only exception is brief quotations in printed reviews. Short excerpts may be used with the publisher's or author's expressed written permission.

Scripture quotations, unless otherwise noted, are from the King James or New King James Versions of the Bible. Scripture taken from the New King James Version. Copyright © 1982 by Thomas Nelson, Inc. Used by permission. All rights reserved.

Ten Words That Will Change Everything You Know About God

Cover and Interior Page design by True Potential, Inc.

ISBN: (Paperback): 9781948794626

ISBN: (e-book): 9781948794633

True Potential, Inc.
PO Box 904, Travelers Rest, SC 29690 www.truepotentialmedia.com

Produced and Printed in the United States of America.

Contents

1. The Veil Over My Heart — 5
2. Becoming One With God — 11
3. Removing the Veil — 17
4. Who's Behind the Veil? — 21
5. The Mind of Christ — 26

SECTION 2 INTRODUCTION: UNRAVELING THE VEIL — **31**

LOVE — **33**

6. Completing the Love of God — 34
7. Love As God Intended — 38

WRATH — **43**

8. Wrath is Rare — 44
9. How can a God of Love Have Wrath? — 47

CHASTISEMENT — **51**

10. Like the Twinkling of an Eye — 52
11. Chastisement By Grace — 54

CURSE — **59**

12. Cursed in Our Own Strength — 60
13. The Curse Without Cause Does Not Come — 62

CONNECTION — **69**

14. God Wants to Give You a Kiss — 70
15. The Mystery of Transformation — 73

JUDGMENT — **79**

16. Every Act Brings Itself into Judgment — 80

17. Peace Through Judgment	82
GRACE	**89**
18. Pitching a Tent in God's Camp	90
19. Grace and Peace	93
FAITH	**97**
20. Works Are Built into Faith	98
21. Trusting God	102
SHALOM	**109**
22. Peace Perfected	110
23. Peace That Defies Circumstances	113
YOKE	**119**
24. A Picture of Satisfaction and Contentment	120
25. Harmonizing With God	123
WHAT NOW?	**129**
26. What Now?	130

Chapter 1

THE VEIL OVER MY HEART

We tend to understand God in a way that justifies our intentions!

There are two unique situations where people came to Jesus and asked, "What must I do to inherit eternal life?" One of these occasions prompted Jesus to share the parable of the Good Samaritan, which has been eloquently preached for centuries. Many wonderful life lessons have come from this parable, but there are three factors seldom discussed: 1) What was the question that caused Jesus to launch into this story? 2) Why did the man ask the question? 3) What can I learn from these two questions?

"And behold, a certain lawyer stood up and tested Him, saying, 'Teacher, what shall I do to inherit eternal life?'" (Luke 10:25-26). Jesus did something we should all do when asked a question, especially a spiritual question: be sure we understand the question! Words are the basis of nearly all communication. Even that which is communicated by images and pictures will eventually be understood and explained in words.

A naïve tendency is to think that because we speak the same language, using the same words, we must share the same definitions… right? Not only is that nearly never true, but there are few places where it will be more untrue than when discussing the Bible.

Redefining words is one of the most subtle tactics for twisting the truth. Once a person accepts or assumes a specific definition for a word, every time that word is heard, it evokes those specific thoughts, emotions, and concepts. I have seen violent arguments erupt because one person, rather than asking for clarification, erupted into violence because of the interpretation of what was said, based on an incorrect meaning of words.

All words have a different history with every individual. I grew up in Tennessee in the 1950s–1960s. We all called one another "boys." Then, in the '60s, at the height of the racial conflicts, we moved to Birmingham, Alabama, a hotbed of racism and riots.

> They think they're right, but inwardly they know something is missing.

I didn't grow up in racism, knew very little about racial conflict; I was entirely ignorant and naïve about all things racial until I referred to a group of guys on the playground as "boys." Even though there were whites in the group, the black boys became angry and hostile. I had no idea what was happening. I didn't know what that term meant to them. All their lives they had seen their fathers and grandfathers referred to as "boys," which meant they were never seen as men. It was incredibly insulting!

Rather than assuming what the expert in the law meant, Jesus asked him an amazing question, *"He said to him, 'What is written in the law? What is your reading of it?'"* (Luke 10:26). The lawyer answered, *"You shall love the Lord your God with all your heart, with all your soul, with all your strength, and with all your mind,' and 'your neighbor as yourself."* (vs. 27)

This is the answer that any good Jew would have given, which begs two questions, "If you knew the answer, why did you ask the question?" and "If you knew the answer, what was your real intention?" We know from the Scripture that this man wasn't looking for answers; he was testing Jesus. Despite the man's duplicitous motive, Jesus did what God always does, "No matter why you're here, I'm going to turn this into an opportunity to help you!"

Jesus replies in verse 28, *"You have answered rightly; do this and you will live."* Remember Jesus' original question, "What does the Bible say, and how do you read it?" He was asking this man how he was interpreting what he was reading.

This religious legalist is just like every fool who wants to argue. They think they're right, but inwardly they know something is missing. If they had a deep sense of wholeness, they wouldn't need to argue. If their hearts were at peace, they wouldn't be troublemakers; they'd be peacemakers! So, he asks one more question that reveals his need, *"But he, wanting to justify himself, said to Jesus, "And who is my neighbor?"* (vs. 29)

Operating through what many would call a "word of knowledge," Jesus followed the Holy Spirit into the perfect life-lesson to help this man. As I've discovered in ministry, over nearly half-a-century: the truth with the most potential to set you free is the truth with the most potential to offend you. Why? When we experience lack in any area, it's always due to an aspect of God's Word we don't know or don't want to know! When challenged by the truth, we either resist or repent.

This lawyer was a racist—a "spiritual-elitist." He had a "black hole" in his heart that made it impossible to love his neighbor as himself, especially if a Samaritan was his neighbor. Up until this moment, he was able to read the scripture commanding him to love his neighbor as himself and interpret it in a way that exempted him from loving a Samaritan.

The Apostle Paul made an insightful statement about his ministry to the Corinthians. He explained, *"God made us ministers of the new covenant, not of the letter but of the Spirit; for the letter kills, but the Spirit gives life."* (2 Cor. 3:6) At first glance, this seems to be a simple comparison between the Old and New Covenants, but it goes much deeper!

The Scriptures from which the apostles preached is what we call *The Old Testament*. The truth is, there's no such thing as *The Old Testament*, as it relates to the Scripture. This is one of those places where religious leaders redefined words in an attempt to alienate Christians from Scriptures that revealed God's true character and nature. I'm thankful for what the apostles wrote, but they'd be appalled to know their teaching had been used to bring about the rejection of the very Words spoken by God Himself!

One of the significant changes from the Old Covenant to the New Covenant was the mode of communication between God and man. The truth of God's Word didn't change. Everything Jesus and the apostles taught was based on the Old Testament; the difference was that it was modeled and taught from God's original intention when He spoke those words.

He uses the story of Moses covering his face, after coming down from the mountain with God, to emphasize an important fact. Moses asked to see God's glory. Amazingly, God didn't express His unlimited power; He didn't move a mountain or create signs in the heavens. He revealed His goodness to Moses. While there is more to this than I'm writing, the root Hebrew Word *glory* is spelled Kap כ Bet ב Dalet ד. This reveals that Moses wanted to see what would happen when a human being emptied his heart and allowed God to fill it so he could enter through the portal into God's love and presence.

This is why God showed His goodness. The Hebrew indicates that God revealed the incredible, beautiful pleasure we can experience when we harmonize our heart with His. Moses is so engulfed in how good God is, that it shows on his face. He rushes to the bottom of the mountain to share what he had just experienced, but the Israelites refused to see.

Many of the Israelites, and especially the mixed multitudes, clung to their pagan concepts of the gods of Egypt, which they projected onto God. Based on all their other responses to God, I'm sure they would have seen this brilliance as life-threatening. They couldn't look upon it, because, remember, these were the same people who said, "We don't want to talk to God; you talk to Him for us."

Get the picture here: Moses saw something that was virtually unexplainable in words. God couldn't even explain it to him; he had to perceive it. It's important to understand that God didn't explain His goodness to Moses; He caused him to see and experience it. Moses is attempting to put into words that which could not be spoken and comprehended. Then, to add rejection to unbelief, the people didn't even want to see the effect it had on Moses, after which had to cover his face with a veil.

Moses experienced the difficulty of attempting to put into words what he had experienced in his heart. The people, then, interpreted those words based on their perception of God. So, God showed it to Moses. Moses, in turn, attempted to put an unexplainable experience into words, and the people interpreted His words based on their beliefs and limited understanding. You can be sure what they held in their intellectual mind wasn't even close to what Moses experienced with God.

Paul uses this scenario to help us understand the problem with any attempt to perceive God through an intellectual transmission of information, "*But their minds were blinded: for until this day the same veil remains unlifted in the reading of the Old Testament (contract).*" (2 Cor. 3:14) Notice that the problem is not with the Old Testament; the problem is with the **reading** of the Old Testament.

Remember when Jesus asked, *"What does the Scripture say, and how do you read it?"* The problem is never with the Word of God. The problem is how we interpret the Word of God and what we try to make it say. Maybe we're like the lawyer who needed to justify himself based on his interpretation of *"Who is my neighbor?"*

The veil that makes us twist the word is our opinions that come through cultural development, education, family tradition, denominational training, and, more times than not, the need to justify or excuse ungodly behavior. The weakness of the written Word is that it is subject to our interpretation. We can make it almost anything we want it to say.

> The Old and New Covenants have many distinctions but shouldn't be confused with the Old and New Testaments.

The Old and New Covenants have many distinctions but shouldn't be confused with the Old and New Testaments. In the New Covenant, through the new birth, the Holy Spirit comes into our hearts, bringing all of God's Word and all it implies,

> *For this is the covenant that I will make with the house of Israel after those days, says the Lord: I will put My laws in their mind and write them on their hearts, and I will be their God, and they shall be My people.* (Heb. 8:10)

Before the new birth, God spoke to us through angels, prophets, and various other means, but in this covenant, He speaks to us through His Son (Heb. 1:1-2)! This verse tells us many important things, but the most significant is this: He reveals everything to us through Jesus: His life, ministry, death, burial, and resurrection. The second most important thing is that He does so through the Holy Spirit, in our heart, not through our "reading of it (interpretation)," but by the Great Teacher, i.e., the Holy Spirit.

Reading the word renews our mind; it gives us the information we need. Then, we interpret everything God has ever said through what we see in Jesus life, teaching, and the cross. The Holy Spirit personally guides us through how to apply the word to our life. The writer of Hebrews is clear: no one can teach you to experience God, because experiencing God occurs through personal involvement, *"None of them shall teach his neighbor, and none his brother, saying, 'Know the Lord,' for all shall know Me, from the least of them to the greatest of them."* (Heb 8:11)

Only God can teach us what we need, but to perceive His teaching, we must remove the veil that distorts how we see and interpret Him.

Chapter 2

BECOMING ONE WITH GOD

Removing the veil starts with the intention of being one with God through Jesus!

Being one with God is when the opinions of our mind, the beliefs of our heart, and the actions that express those beliefs are based on the Word of God as taught and modeled by Jesus… the Messiah! Harmony should be the goal of every believer! Our problem, however, is we're not fully convinced God can and will fulfill our desires. Consequently, we create a veil, a way of perceiving and interpreting God's Word so that it says what we need it to say.

What starts out as mere compromises and justifications become a trap of thoughts and beliefs making it seemingly impossible to perceive God in any other manner. Our limiting beliefs not only lead to a life void of power but settling for a lesser quality of life than Jesus died to give us!

The problem with how we read the word is two-fold: the mind and the heart. The **mind** is *the seat of intellectual learning.* This intellectualism is ego-driven. The **ego** is *our false sense of self.* This sense of self is based on being right. Our mind primarily seeks to protect our ego by always proving we're right; therefore, the mind evaluates and interprets all incoming data on previous experiences and opinions. The mind works on the basis of information and emotions.[1]

---
1   Jim Richards, *Moving Your Invisible Boundaries* (Travelers Rest: True Potential, 2013)

The heart, on the other hand, seeks to establish our identity based on beliefs and feelings. Beliefs emerge from a combination of the information we believe to be true, and how that information defines us. From this sense of self, we interpret God and the world. The **heart**—*our sense of self*—is *the seat of our morals, values, and ethics.* The Bible credits the heart with our capacity for wisdom and understanding. It's these beliefs that form the boundaries that comprise the limitations or the limitlessness of our life!

In 2 Corinthians 3:14-15, Paul explains how the veil keeps us from seeing God as He is, due to a combination of what's happening in both our mind and heart, *"But their minds were blinded. For until this day the same veil remains unlifted in the reading of the Old Testament… But even to this day, when Moses is read, a veil lies on their heart."*

> The way we think can't be driven by the need to be right, to protect our ego or for personal gain.

The Bible teaches us to renew our minds. For many, that's nothing more than gathering new information. But if we gather new information and assess it based on faulty beliefs, we'll read (interpret) that information to say what we want or need it to say to protect our ego! New information never means a change in perspective.

Renewing the mind, from a Biblical perspective, not only requires new information (what we think) but a new attitude and a change in how we think. In Philippians, Paul tells us how to think,

> *Fulfill my joy by being like-minded, having the same love, being of one accord, of one mind. Let nothing be done through selfish ambition or conceit, but in lowliness of mind let each esteem others better than himself. Let each of you look out not only for his own interests, but also for the interests of others. Let this mind be in you which was also in Christ Jesus." (Phil 2:2-5)*

The way we think can't be driven by the need to be right, to protect our ego or for personal gain. If we're to be one with God, through the Lord Jesus, we must think with the motive and intentions He displayed. ***Renewing the mind*** is *harmonizing with God in what we think, how we think, and the intentions that drive our thoughts*!

The mind is the seat of conscious thought, but the heart is the source from which subconscious thought emerges. The mind operates in the continuum of emotions, but the heart operates through the continuum of feelings. Emotions follow conscious thought. When we focus our conscious attention on anything, the mind, through the nervous system (flesh), creates emotions. Emotions come quickly, and spike quickly, but can be changed just as quickly. All that's required to change our emotions is to think about or focus on something different!

Feelings, however, are linked to beliefs of the heart. They emerge slowly; in fact, so slowly, we seldom realize changes are occurring. With emotions, it's easy to realize that they've changed once we begin thinking about something else. All we have to do is focus our attention elsewhere, and they will change. Feelings, however, emerge so slowly and subtly, it's difficult to determine the place from which they came, or when they began to arise. Deep-seated, heart feelings are not based on momentary conscious thoughts; they're based on our sense of self—our identity!

It's important to realize this crucial difference: In the mind, thoughts give rise to emotions, but, in the heart, it's just the opposite. Feelings give rise to thoughts, which bring forth more emotions. Since our identity is rooted in the beliefs of the heart, it's not a simple matter to change those beliefs.

Since they define our identity, changing the beliefs of the heart is experienced as death, which is exactly what we're experiencing. **Dying-to-self** isn't the suffering religion has imposed upon us; it occurs when we put off the "*old man.*" Transformation and resurrection occur when we renew the mind and put on the "*new man.*" It's this transformation of which Paul speaks in Romans: the death of everything we believe about ourselves and our identity that is not based on our death, burial, and resurrection with Jesus.

Once we've established a sense of self through a lifelong acquisition of beliefs, the heart will do everything it can to protect that false sense of self and the beliefs whereby it was created. It doesn't matter if those beliefs are healing or killing us, the heart preserves them until we use the tools Jesus taught to transform them. This is the ultimate battlefield: the conscious thoughts we choose and the antagonistic resistance from the subconscious thoughts that define us.

Thousands of years of philosophy, therapy, counseling, and positive thinking have proven one thing: When there is a struggle between the conscious and the subconscious, the subconscious always wins... that is, unless you know how to change the beliefs of your heart. You can't "power, will, or think" your way out of the beliefs of your heart.

The sincere efforts of believers to overcome their past and be the person they know they can be, want to be, and should be in Christ, are nearly always thwarted because we ignore Jesus' teaching about influencing and transforming the heart. Endeavoring to consciously discipline one's thoughts is tedious, torturous, and ultimately exhausting. It requires continual effort. All it takes to fall right back into previous patterns of thought, emotions, and subsequent behavior is one moment of not trying hard enough.

Proverbs 17:20 (KJV) says, *"He that hath a froward heart findeth no good."* The word ***froward*** basically means *crooked*.[2] The root word in the Hebrew language points to a problem of perception concerning holiness that consumes us through our passions. It's a heart that can't believe for fulfillment by walking with God. It's a heart with a distorted perception of God and His truth, making it impossible to find good (harmony) with Him and His blessings.

Righteousness is often described as a straight, smooth path that's well-lit and safe to walk. Alternatively, unrighteousness is often described as a crooked path, filled with pitfalls and danger. Proverbs 12:28 emphasizes, *"In the way (path) of righteousness there is life and no death."* A crooked heart is like one side of a railroad track that begins to veer out of alignment (harmony) with the other track, causing the train to derail, bringing death and destruction. Yoking up with Jesus requires harmony, i.e., keeping in step. In other words, the track He's running on and the track we're running on must be aligned.

A crooked heart—a heart that doesn't see God as He is—distorts our capacity to understand the Word of God and see Him as He is. No matter how hard we may try to change our intellectual concepts, we won't see or experience God as He is until we change our heart beliefs.

The problem with a crooked heart is that it bends everything it hears and sees to match its shape. Light changes color when it's bent. It's still light,

---

2   OT:6141 `iqqesh (ik-kashe'); from OT:6140; distorted; hence, false: - crooked, froward, perverse; Biblesoft, *Strong's Concordance* (Online: Biblesoft, 2006)

but it's not clear light nor does it clearly illuminate the path. When we read or hear God's Word, the light that could come to us is bent. We may get some of it; we may even experience some benefit, but we never really perceive it for what it is. Even the meaning of what God speaks directly into our heart is bent to preserve the way we need to understand it; thus, if we ignore Jesus' instruction about how to transform our beliefs and establish our heart, no matter how hard we try we end up back at the same place, with the same old beliefs and the same old problems. It's like living in the endless loop of the *Twilight Zone*, repeating the same day over and over.

> Prayer only occurs from a heart that's open to Jesus and ready to be taught.

If we desire to see God as He is and live the quality of life He promised, it's incumbent upon us to follow what the Bible teaches from the beginning… believe the truth in our heart. In the parable of the seed, Jesus taught how to establish the Word of God in our heart. To the degree of thought, study, pondering, considering, and meditating we give to the Word we hear, determines the quality and quantity of the fruit it produces in our life. To have what Jesus promised, we must choose the harvest we want, plant the seed (truth) that will produce that type of fruit, cultivate the soil of our heart, and nurture the seed with meditation. Then, we must stop planting opposing seed (thorns) that chokes out the Word.

As we read the Word of God, we should do so in prayer and meditation. Prayer only occurs from a heart that's open to Jesus and ready to be taught. Meditation is when we envision what that Word would be when applied to our life until we experience it as being real in our heart. What would we look like and feel like if we were actually experiencing the Word as Jesus taught it and as He ministered it? This is the process of renewing the mind and influencing the heart.

The first, and most noticeable, way of knowing when a heart belief has been changed is that, once established, it requires no conscious effort to perform. The second way to know is that it alters the way we perceive and experience ourselves. Beliefs make new truth seem easy and light, i.e., effortless! When truth becomes a belief of the heart, all wrestling with the conscious mind or mustering the discipline to keeps one's self under control ends! Through my **Heart Physics Program,** I've created what I call: positive, painless, permanent, and effortless transformation. For more information, please visit: www.HeartPhysics.com.

We must begin our heart transformation with the intention to harmonize our beliefs and become one with God; but, before this is possible, we must understand the most crucial part: removing the veil!

Chapter 3

REMOVING THE VEIL

Being In Christ is nothing more than information … until faith and intention are applied!

Jesus drove the religious community crazy by demonstrating and teaching that He was one with God. Fully accepting this truth and allowing it to become our basis for relating to God, our Father, is the basis for perceiving God as He is.

We all know Jesus came to give us the abundant life (John 10:10), but we fail to grasp what participating in that abundant life means and involves. As I've discussed in many of my writings, the life of Jesus offers us the same quality of life He received from the Father.

We tend to think of this life of God as a tangible object He gives to us, but it's not; it's something only experienced through personal involvement with God via the Lord Jesus. *"And this is eternal life, that they may know You, the only true God, and Jesus Christ whom You have sent."* (John 17:3) We can only experience God as He is when we experience Him as Jesus demonstrated He is. Any perception of God other than what Jesus revealed through His life, teachings, ministry, death, burial, and resurrection is a vain imagination opposing the revealed knowledge of God!

A Jew I once ministered to in our community was very open to what I shared. But I was taken back when he explained, "The reason I won't listen to other Christians is because all they talk about is Jesus; they never talk about God."

That conversation sparked me to have conversations with many of my Christians friends and what I discovered was shocking. They all knew they had to believe on Jesus to be saved but had very little idea how Jesus really factored into our ability to know God. Part of the problem was in their definition of the word *know*. The general consensus was something like this, "If I believe on Jesus, the door will be open for Him to make the introduction between me and the Father." It was as if Jesus was nothing more than the legal passage-way providing access to God! All of the above is true, but it's by no means the fullness of what we have in Jesus.

> They wanted a god in their own image. Then, they twisted His Words to mean something completely different than His intentions when He spoke them.

The ultimate failure of Israel as a nation was unbelief, not a general unbelief, but the unbelief concerning the true character and nature of God. God was never holy to them as a nation. The opposite of **holiness** is *common*. God was uncommon, unlike any of the gods of the world. He was a relational God whose every action was based on His love for mankind: completely uncommon! His desire was for them to see Him as He is, trust him to form a relationship with Him so they could experience His goodness, whereby they too would become uncommon among all the peoples of the world!

Instead of taking God at His Word, they twisted the image of the Living God to be like the nature of the pagan gods. They wanted a god that fulfilled their lusts and fit into their religious paradigms. They wanted a god in their own image. Then, they twisted His Words to mean something completely different than His intentions when He spoke them. Ultimately, they morphed into the image of God they projected onto Him through their crooked hearts! Religion has so corrupted the character and nature of God that, to this day, the church still sees the commandments as negative and destructive.

When Jesus came into the world, the Bible says, *"And the Word became flesh and dwelt among us, and we beheld His glory, the glory as of the only begotten of the Father, full of grace and truth."* (John 1:14) Part of Jesus' mission on earth was to reveal the glory of God, whose glory was manifest in grace, truth, and goodness.

God told Moses He would pass before Him and reveal His glory. It's important to realize that God didn't reveal curses, earthquakes, or vengeance; He revealed His goodness. God's goodness is a manifestation of His greatness. Jesus came to show us in human form, on Planet Earth, the true character and nature of God... as it always has been.

In 2 Corinthians 3:16, Paul declares, *"Nevertheless when one turns to the Lord, the veil is taken away."* The accepted interpretation of this passage is, "I'm saved, so the veil is taken away from my eyes." Sadly, not only is that a flawed interpretation of what is being stated, it's simply not reality for most Christians. It seems that Christians in general have a difficult time reconciling what they believe to be the difference between the God of "Old Testament" and Jesus. Why? The eyes of their heart are still blinded in the way they read, or their pastor reads, the "Old Testament." They still interpret the Old Testament as religion has done since Moses came down from the mountain!

Until we look at Jesus and agree that He is the exact representation of who God is and who God has always been, the veil has not been taken away from our heart (Heb. 1:3)! We're failing to grasp one of the primary goals of Jesus coming to earth: revealing the glory of the Father!

When Jesus made statements, such as, *"I and the Father are one."* (John 10:30), *"The words that I speak to you I do not speak on my own authority."* (John 14:10), and *"I only do the works I see my Father doing."* (John 5:19), were a direct challenge to the religious powerbrokers who were presenting a different concept of God. Religious leaders always present an image of God that makes us think we need them to be our mediator. True servants of God, are leaders who point you to total reliance on the One True God you can know, trust, and experience because you've seen Him in Jesus!

One powerful dynamic presented in the Scripture occurs from beholding God as the power of transformation. I say it like this, "You become what you behold." The Psalms are full of descriptions of what happens in the presence of God, but the Apostle John probably said it best, *"We shall be like Him, for we shall see Him as He is."* (1 John 3:2) Transformation occurs when we see God as He is and as we interpret His every Word and action based on Jesus' portrayal of Him.

Faith in Jesus isn't just the belief that He existed. It's also more than believing He did all that the Gospels record that He did; it's believing He is

God in the flesh, doing and saying exactly what God the Father would do and say if He were here. Jesus never made a well person sick, and He never used harm, guilt or fear to influence people to follow Him. He demonstrated the love of God. His only harsh words were to the religious leaders who distorted God's image and led believers into captivity.

Paul explained that we're all removing the veil in degrees. To the degree we accept Jesus' witness of God is the degree to which we go through the process of seeing God as He is—knowing Him through Jesus and experiencing transformation into the likeness we perceive, *"But we all, with unveiled face, beholding as in a mirror the glory of the Lord, are being transformed into the same image from glory to glory, just as by the Spirit of the Lord."* (2 Cor 3:18)

Chapter 4

WHO'S BEHIND THE VEIL

I want God to be like me, so I can feel good about me!

One of the greatest struggles between God and mankind has been our self-induced incapacity and even defiant unwillingness to see God as He is. The world doesn't want to perceive a moral, ethical, loving God. To do so would create moral absolutes. The wickedness of the world could no longer be justified. Maintaining a negative concept of God justifies rejecting Him and His commandments as oppressive. Seeing God as He is would destroy the control mechanism put in place by those who, through their lust for power, are the true oppressors of mankind!

Isaiah 53, the chapter that foretells Jesus' death on the cross, opens with one of the most important questions in the Bible, *"Who has believed our report?"* From Adam in the Garden to the 21st century person on the street, there's been resistance in our hearts to believe God is who He proclaims Himself to be. However passive and polite we may be in our disbelief, it's still tantamount to calling God a liar!

In the Garden, Adam and Eve lived in a paradise, unparalleled by man's best efforts throughout history to reproduce it. Their every need was met; they lacked for nothing. Sin, sickness, disease, fear, and lack were nonexistent. In this state of continual provision and protection, they allowed themselves to be beguiled. The original temptation seductively led them to three false and destructive conclusions: 1) We're not like God, and

2) God isn't who He claims to be; therefore, 3) God can't be trusted. From these conclusions, sin and death entered the earth and reigned in the hearts of men, resulting in spiritual, emotional, and physical death!

Lying at the heart of every problem in the world is the refusal to believe: 1) We're created in the likeness and image of God, 2) God is whom He revealed Himself to be through His names, His Word, and the life, teaching, death, burial and resurrection of Jesus, and 3) God is faithful and trustworthy to uphold His every word. There's no other cause for destruction in the world. There's no mystery to solve!

> Because we don't see God as He is, we can never see and experience ourselves as we truly are—as God created us!

Our beliefs concerning the nature of God and our own identity follow a continuum. Because we don't see God as He is, we can never see and experience ourselves as we truly are—as God created us! Based on a distorted sense of self, we create an image of God that harmonizes with the way we perceive ourselves. In other words, we reverse the reality. Instead of believing God created us in His likeness and image, we create an idolatrous misrepresentation of God in our perceived likeness and image: an endless cycle leading to an unending disconnect between God and us. Only one solution for the sinister syndrome of unbelief and destruction exists: We must see God as He is! We must believe His report!

Isaiah 52:5-9 presents a clear statement of the need to see God as He is: *"'Now, therefore, what have I here,' says the Lord, 'That My people are taken away for nothing?'"* (vs. 5) He's saying there's no reason His people (the Israelites) should have been taken into captivity and oppressed; yet they were led captive by the pagan nations of the world, where they suffered slavery, persecution, and torture.

He goes on to say, *"'Those who rule over them make them wail.'"* (vs. 5) It's not God making them wail and moan; it's their oppressors. Like most humans, we blame God for the consequences of our foolishness. As Proverbs so aptly points out, *"The foolishness of a man twists his way, And his heart frets against the Lord."* (19:3)

God continues His declaration, *"And My name is blasphemed continually every day."* (vs. 5) All over the world, leaders, parents, couples, and individuals make horrible decisions, never considering the outcome. Then, when suffering arises, they blame God for not delivering them. Christians ignore the wisdom of God's Word, harden their hearts to the leadership of the Holy Spirit for important life lessons, and, in many cases, willfully violate God's Word to fulfill their own lusts (desires). Upon suffering the consequences of those choices, they too blaspheme God by blaming Him for their suffering.

God promises that a day will come when people will know His identity because they'll believe in His name. His name was the clearest testimony of His character and nature prior to Jesus' coming. Had Israel chosen to use God's names as the basis for interpreting His Word, they would have never reached such corrupt, legalistic interpretations and applications of the commandments, *"Therefore My people shall know My name; Therefore they shall know in that day that I am He who speaks: 'Behold, it is I.'"* (vs. 6)

The following passage provides incredible insight to understanding and perceiving God as He really is. It's the revelation that changes everything we think we know about God. Here's what those who believe God's Word will say upon accepting God's testimony of Himself:

> *How beautiful upon the mountains are the feet of him who brings good news, Who proclaims peace, Who brings glad tidings of good things, Who proclaims salvation, Who says to Zion, "Your God reigns!" Your watchmen shall lift up their voices, With their voices they shall sing together; For they shall see eye to eye.* (vs. 7-8)

Paul repeats this passage in Romans 10:15, *"How beautiful are the feet of those who preach the gospel of peace."* The gospel of peace is the message of the New Covenant established in Jesus, which Isaiah identifies as the covenant of peace (Isa. 54:10). After suffering all the consequences of sin for the entire world, God made a covenant of peace with Jesus. Those who believe in Jesus as Lord are baptized into His body, becoming one with Him, thereby, sharing in His covenant of peace with God. We, who are in Jesus, receive from God what is given to Jesus.

Paul repeats in his epistle to the Roman believers the words of Isaiah, *"For 'the name of God is blasphemed among the Gentiles because of you,' as it is written."* (Rom 2:24) It seems the greatest destruction to God's reputation has always been those who call themselves by His name, specifically those who proclaim the "angry-God" message, directly opposing the Good News (gospel).

When we use Jesus as our looking-glass into the heart of God, we see behind the veil. If Jesus is the perfect representation of God, we don't see an angry judgmental God; we see our Creator and Father who deeply loves and adores us. We discover He is both preemptive and proactive in His love. He created a world specifically designed to sustain life at its highest possible capacity. He placed man in paradise with absolutely no lack. Eden was the perfect expression of God's will for us.

> God provided the ultimate sacrificial expression of love: sending His Son to die and deliver mankind from the consequences of sin.

When man destroyed paradise, God didn't abandon him to his own selfish devices. Instead, He provided instructions for how to live in a world that had fallen under the influence of sin and death. Those who gave themselves fully to the idolatrous immorality of worshipping false gods, had surrendered to Lucifer and sought to overthrow the world and God by building a tower. In their quest, they discovered secrets to manipulate the natural power of the world (that still can't be comprehended). God divided the languages to keep this occult knowledge from total world annihilation.

When the world rejected the wisdom of God handed down from the Garden, He provided a moral prescription (the commandments) for health, happiness, social, and civil justice. In man's attempt to make God like all the pagan gods, he twisted God's prescriptions for life into legalistic, deathly misrepresentations, leading to the destruction of their nation.

When the greatest code for human dignity—liberating women and slaves, providing true civil justice, preventing the wealthy from oppressing the poor—was ignored, God provided the ultimate sacrificial expression of love: sending His Son to die and deliver mankind from the consequences of sin. He made it impossible for anyone to misunderstand the intentions behind His every Word and deed.

In less than one generation, the human, religious race had rejected the Scriptures that foretold of the New Covenant and turned to cult and occult mysticism as a means of interpreting Jesus' sacrifice. For the most part, mankind has ignored and rejected His salvation. Yet, He has never repented of His love for the human race. He prepared and promised His intervention once again to deliver the earth from the wickedness that will arise from man's harmonious romance with Satan's life principles.

Jesus will return to rule the world in righteousness. When the largest population of the world exists, and most are deceived, Jesus will return to reign on earth for 1,000 years to demonstrate how wonderful life on earth could have been had we trusted Him and applied His truth. This will prove to all mankind that God's testimony of Himself is true so as many as possible will come to Him.

The veil over our hearts alters our perception of God, thereby altering how we read (interpret) and apply God's Word. Until that veil is removed from our hearts, we can't see Him as He is; therefore, we can never believe in His goodness and willingness to meet our every need, resulting in our limited capacity to experience Him fully!

This book: ***Ten Words That Will Change Everything You Know About God***, provides you with the tools to help remove the veil to see God clearly. The more you see Him as He is, the more you remove all the limits imposed upon us by religion, culture, and the world's system.

Who's behind the veil? The God, who loves us more than we've ever imagined, who has a better life for us than we've ever seen, heard or imagined. He awaits eagerly for us to draw near to Him and partake of all He's provided!

Chapter 5

THE MIND OF CHRIST

I only have the mind of Christ when I believe about God what He believed!

In the Garden, it seems that communication was more internal, whereas, after the fall, it became more verbal and intellectual. It may be that, because of its dependence on the brain and nervous system, verbal communication is part of the continuum of the flesh. This could explain why, *"The letter kills, but the Spirit gives life."* (2 Cor. 3:6, NASB)

We can't, however, reject the benefits that come from a mind surrendered to the Spirit of God. The mind itself isn't evil, but the carnal mind is death.

> *For to be carnally minded is death, but to be spiritually minded is life and peace. Because the carnal mind is enmity against God; for it is not subject to the law of God, nor indeed can be. So then, those who are in the flesh cannot please God.* (Rom. 8:6-8)

The carnal mind relies on the five senses to take in data from the natural world, which could be based on an emotional aberration. Our mind intellectually assesses input based on our life experiences. The brain follows by stimulating hormones making us feel something as the result of our conclusion. The entire process is based on natural (carnal) capabilities and is subject to the lust of the eyes, the lust of the flesh, and the pride of life!

So, how do we know when we're spiritually minded? For most, it's a subjective determination based on this carnal process. The only difference may be found in trying to find scriptures that seem to validate our opinion. There may be, however, a better way to ensure we're not deceiving ourselves.

The Apostle Paul made an interesting statement, *"For 'who has known the mind of the Lord that he may instruct Him?' But we have the mind of Christ."* (1 Cor. 2:16) I've heard this scripture quoted in bizarre ways. The most common idea is to assume that because we're saved, we think like Jesus. That theory absolutely cannot be proven by observing the average believer!

No one has seen inside the mind of the Father except the Son, *"No one has seen God at any time. The only begotten Son, who is in the bosom of the Father, He has declared Him."* (John 1:18) For thousands of years, God's Words and actions have been interpreted by men who weren't born again and certainly had never seen God. It was this carnal reading of the letter of the law that took what God had given for our benefit and turned it into death!

The original Hebrew alphabet was a set of pictures, which meant they were understood more in concepts than in intellectual explanations. It's worth noting that when the scribes created the block alphabet, it seems they attempted to give those letters the same meanings as the previous images. While those images had meanings, those meanings could have a light side and a dark side. In other words, how they're interpreted is based on the heart beliefs of the person interpreting them. When our image of God is positive, healthy, safe, and is based on Jesus, we'll interpret these meanings in a positive, life-giving way. Conversely, if we hold a negative, pagan view of God, we'll translate His Word and life negatively, legalistically, and or in some other way that produces death!

Our wisdom can't grasp God's Word. This is why God gave us a way to interpret His Word that produces trust. In the Old Testament, He gave His names, which reveal His true character and nature. They could have served as an interpretive logic for everything God ever said or did... if we had been willing to consider them!

In the New Covenant, we have an insight into understanding God and His Word that no other group of people has ever known. It's essential to know a person's character, morals, ethics, attitudes, behavioral tendencies, and thought patterns when attempting to understand what someone is saying. We should also know the person's attitude toward us. If a gangster turns to someone and says, "We've gotta take care of that guy!" It probably means someone is going to die. If a loving Father says about his child, "We've gotta take care of him." it probably means he wants to protect him.

When trying to understand what God means in His Word, we have to know His character and His disposition towards us. Jesus made that possible by perfectly representing Him. He modeled God's and His disposition toward us. We can't attach any interpretation to anything God has ever said or done in a manner that contradicts Jesus or His life, ministry, death, burial, and resurrection.

Through Jesus' teaching, we have the ultimate filter for translating, interpreting, and applying the Word of God.

> *"You shall love the Lord your God with all your heart, with all your soul, and with all your mind." This is the first and great commandment. And the second is like it: "You shall love your neighbor as yourself." On these two commandments hang all the Law and the Prophets.* (Matt. 22:37-40)

> He's given us the Holy Spirit as a Teacher, Guide, and Comforter.

God isn't a hypocrite; He lives what He preaches. He reveals His character and nature so we can live as He does. The way He tells us to treat one another is based on the way He treats us. The way we interpret the scriptures must result in a greater understanding and capacity to love God, love our neighbor, and love ourselves. To interpret it any other way is a rejection of Jesus' life and teachings!

God's names and Jesus' life, death, burial, and resurrection should be more than enough to ensure we truly see God as He is, but He doesn't stop there. He's given us the Holy Spirit as a Teacher, Guide, and Comforter. If we're open and listening, He'll bring His Word and example of Jesus to our mind so we always see God as He is and interpret and apply His Word accordingly.

The last obstacle to seeing God as He is may be the words themselves. Religionists, socialists, pagans, scientists, and humanists unite to twist God's Word into a negative, nonsensical and totally contradictory fashion so that we either reject it or twist it to support our ideology.

The Bibles we read were translated by men and women, probably good men and women that, sadly, never saw God. Naturally, their translations and interpretations are no replacement for what Jesus revealed and manifested! Early English translations have deliberate omissions, additions, and mistranslations that protect the doctrine embraced by the church and government of that time. To make matters worse, the archaic language of the King James Version, and other versions as well, are lost in this generation. The words no longer mean what they meant when these translations were penned. Granted, any serious Bible student who believes what is obviously portrayed by the life and death of Jesus can navigate around these issues unscathed, but many people don't have the time or resources for in-depth Bible study.

The final factor is this: it's not enough that we refuse to study the letter of God's Word, but how do we know what the Spirit is saying? My Hebrew teacher, Chaim Bentorah, teaches that, after going through all the responsible processes of Bible translation, the most important part is to determine what God is speaking to our heart.

Ironically, as a teacher, little of Jesus' teaching ministry was about explaining doctrine. It was all about application… not legalistic obedience. Wisdom, although it has many levels of meaning, is always expressed by practical application. Jesus primarily taught in parables that revealed the applicable wisdom of God's Word. Vital theological concepts are grasped in our heart when we desire to walk in love.

The Holy Spirit helps us understand how to apply God's Word into our lives, in every unique set of circumstances we face. Plus, He manifests the **grace**, i.e., *the capacity, ability, and strength*, to follow through with His guidance. Application should be motivated by love and, at the end of the process, should reveal the love of God to those to who are affected by our actions so they will see God as He is!

In this book, Chaim Bentorah and I provide more biblically-based translations, interpretations, and some applications for key words that have been mistranslated, misinterpreted, and misapplied for centuries and in some cases, millennia. We provide sound interpretations that reflect the character and nature of God as represented by His names, as well as the life, teaching, ministry, death, burial, and resurrection of Jesus.

By choosing to see God as He is, you can experience effortless transformation into the way you perceive God. As you discover more accurate translations of God's Word, you'll soon realize that you read, understand, and apply God's Word differently, because you now see Him with the mind of Christ!

Section 2

INTRODUCTION
UNRAVELING THE VEIL

The veil distorting our view of God is comprised of personal opinions and beliefs of the heart. When our opinions are questioned, it usually threatens our ego. When our beliefs are challenged, we can literally become unable to hear, perceive, understand, and ultimately believe what's being said, unless we have a repentant, teachable heart!

For the teachable, the journey from unbelief to trusting God's report of Himself is still quite a challenging journey. When, however, we learn how to apply Jesus' teaching for influencing our heart (from the parable of the sower), it can happen painlessly and quickly!

The veil that alters our perception is a tapestry representing a life paradigm through which we interpret everything we see, hear, and experience. The strands of the fabric are beliefs, like spooled cotton woven together comprising the fabric of the veil. The individual fibers spooled together create threads. How tightly the threads are woven is the degree to which we believe and apply faulty doctrine. The stronger the beliefs, the harder it is to see through the tightly woven fabric and actually perceive God as He is!

Sometimes, the easiest way to unravel a faulty belief is by looking at individual words. Discovering a proper biblical definition of a word can be like picking at a thread on a sweater; when you pull on it, the entire sweater starts to unravel. Words fit together to make statements, and statements comprise ideals, which lead to opinions and ultimately, beliefs. Each word properly defined makes it harder to hold to a false statement.

In this next section, I've selected ten words for which their improper definitions, interpretations, and subsequent applications may have caused you to see God in a negative light or even made it impossible to see just how good God really is. Religion is like a crooked prosecutor who exaggerates any possible negatives about a person and withholds exculpatory evidence in an attempt to cause the jury to find the defendant guilty.

In light of the skewed evidence presented and the exculpatory evidence withheld, many innocent victims have been found guilty. Likewise, God's been found guilty of murder, oppression, thievery, and sadism. Unfortunately, the father of lies knows, the more a lie is repeated, the more people believe it to be true, even in the face of overwhelming facts to the contrary.

As you read the following pages, you'll be faced with one foundational question, "Do I want to see God as He is or do I want God to be who I already perceive Him to be?" I'd highly recommend answering that question before proceeding.

If you're challenged by the definitions of the following words, do your homework. Look at the sources quoted. Prayerfully consider the logic that emerges when you free your mind from the faulty logic of religion that perverts the way you see God.

Remember, the law of transformation teaches that you become like the God in which you believe. If you desire to be more like Jesus, experience more of the fruit of the Spirit and have greater influence on the world, you must see God as He is!

LOVE

Love is the core of our being, the seat of our self-worth, and the foundation for emotional stability.

Chapter 6

COMPLETING THE LOVE OF GOD

(Chaim Bentorah)

John 3:16: *"For God so loved the world, that he gave his only begotten Son, that whosoever believeth in him should not perish, but have everlasting life."*

John 21:20: *"Then Peter, turning about, seeth the disciple whom Jesus loved following; which also leaned on his breast at supper, and said, 'Lord, which is he that betrayeth thee?'"*

We are all familiar with the three words in Greek expressing three levels of love, *Agape (unconditional love), Phileo (brotherly love, friendship)* and *Eros (erotic love).*

Hebrew actually has four words for love, but they are not always translated as love. There is *Ahav (love), Racham (tender mercies), Dodi (beloved, as spousal love),* and *Ra'ah (brotherly love, or friendship).*

It would be wrong to try and make a parallel between the Greek words for love and the Hebrew words for love. This creates a real problem in translation, as *love* is at the very root and center of Scripture. I suppose we could say that the closest to *Ahav* is Agape, *Ra'ah* is like *Phileo,* and *Dodi* is like *Eros.* Yet, this would not be accurate, as *Ahav* is used in cases where *Agape* would not fit, *Ra'ah,* although rendered as friendship, is also rendered as Shepherd and consuming passion, and is often used by David to express his love for God, so it would be inappropriate to consider *Ra'ah* as equivalent to *Phileo* in many cases. *Dodi* is used by Solomon toward his beloved to express a sexual desire, but it does not carry the lustful, self-gratification of *Eros*.

There is a fourth word in Hebrew for love, and that is *Racham*, which is often expressed as romantic love, or rendered as *tender mercies*. It is rarely used in the Old Testament, but is frequently found in the Aramaic New Testament where it is spelled the same and sounds the same as it does in Hebrew.

In the Greek New Testament, we find that the word used for *love* in John 3:16 is *Agape*. In the Peshitta, or the Aramaic Bible, it is the word *Chav*, which is similar to the Hebrew word *Ahav*, and means *love*. However, in John 21:20, where we read about the disciple whom Jesus *loved*, the Greek uses, *Agape*, but the Peshitta uses the Aramaic word *Racham*, which is identical to the Hebrew *Racham*.

We know that Jesus and His disciples did not speak in Greek, but in a Northern Old Galilean dialect of Aramaic. Aramaic is difficult to translate. I believe the original manuscripts of the Gospels were written in Aramaic and translated into Greek about twenty years later. Even if I am wrong and they were originally written in Greek, the writer would still have had to translate his words and those of Jesus directly from the Aramaic. We have Aramaic manuscripts that date earlier than our earliest Greek manuscripts, which were lost around 300 A.D. (interestingly, about the time of Constantine). Still, even if Jesus and His disciples used two different Aramaic words for love, the writer and/or translator putting their words into Greek would have been stuck with only one possible word that would fit, and that would be *Agape*.

So when Jesus said that "God so loved the world," He used the Aramaic word *Chav*, but when speaking of the disciple that He *loved*, He used the word *Racham*. These are two entirely different words, both meaning *love*. The most logical conclusion is that we are dealing with two levels of love; this would suggest that He either loved the world more than His disciple or He loved this disciple more than the world.

Is it true that God loves everyone, but does He have favorites? Did He love Joseph more than me, making him a prime minister, and me a bus driver for the disabled? Did God love Moses more than Miriam and Aaron, speaking face to face with Moses but not with his brother or sister?

Note that John 21:20 does not say the disciple whom Jesus *loved*, but the disciple whom Jesus *loved following*. In Greek and Aramaic, the words are more properly rendered as the disciple whom Jesus loved, *who followed Him*. The world does not follow God, but this disciple did follow Jesus.

The key difference between the words *Chav*, which is used in John 3:16, as God loving the world and *Racham*, as used in John 21:20, of the disciple whom Jesus loved, is that *Chav* is a love that is not necessarily returned. *Chav* is speaking of a love that flows from just one person and is not completed. For love to be completed, it must be returned. *Racham* is a completed love.

> You see, God loves the world, but the world does not love Him in return.

Love can be pretty lonely and painful if it is not returned. A teenage girl can pine over some handsome dude who doesn't even know she is alive; she can feel depressed, sad, and broken-hearted, she can *Chav*. But if that teenage guy looks into her eyes and says: "I love you." She is immediately transported to cloud-nine, where birds sing and flowers bloom again. Love can exist if it is not returned, but it cannot sing until it is shared.

As a pastor, I performed many weddings. I always delighted in watching *Chav* turn into *Racham* as I spoke the words: "I now pronounce you husband and wife." At that moment the reality set in that they had declared to the world that they love each other and are committing their lives to one another. In that declaration, they know that they are truly *loved – Racham*.

You see, God loves the world, but the world does not love Him in return. It is when we love Him in return that His love is complete, it is when we love Him in return that he is able to rejoice over us with singing (Zephaniah 3:17). Salvation is not just about being saved and going to heaven; it is about completing the love that God has for us. It brings joy and celebration to the heart of God.

Why do the angels rejoice over one sinner who repents? The same reason you cry at a wedding; you are rejoicing over seeing the joy of two people (not just one) who have found each other in love, and return that love to one another. The angels rejoice for the same reason people read Jane Austen, Elizabeth Barrett Browning, or Grace Livingstone Hill; they love a romance story, where two people love each other.

It is not that God loves one person more than another. He loves all people equally, it is just that few love Him in return and complete His love, awaken Him in that love, and cause Him to sing with joy in that love.

You and I, frail human beings, can bring joy to the God of the Universe by simply saying: "I love you." Have you told Him today that you love Him? Is God's love for you just *Chav (one-sided)?* Or is it *Racham (completed, shared)?* Do you want to give the all-mighty, all-powerful God a thrill? Tell Him you love Him.

To sign up for Chaim Bentorah's free daily Hebrew Word study, explore his books, and learn more about his in-depth biblical Hebrew online learning platform, please visit: https://www.chaimbentorah.com/

Chapter 7

LOVE AS GOD INTENDED

My definition of love can make me a pervert or a saint!

We would think love should be the easiest topic in the world to discuss. Like all things biblical, however, we soon discover this subject is complicated by the many different personal definitions and concepts believers purport to be its true meaning.

Based on personal definitions, love can lead to fanatical legalism, insisting that loving God is attempting to obey all the rules and regulations embraced by that sect. Some experience deep humiliation and wrong as they put a codependent slant on their concept of love that makes them believe they have the right to "walk all over others" while demanding love. The other codependent extreme is to become "emotional doormats" in an attempt to prove their love. Finally, there are those who condone any lifestyle or sin in the name of love.

Just as with any other subject, using correct biblical terminology without biblical definitions doesn't make the belief or behavior biblical. When applied in a way that's inconsistent with God's instructions and how Jesus demonstrated, it's not true love.

As Chaim pointed out, God's character is rooted in love. The Agape love of the New Testament isn't a term used to describe a relationship; it's used to describe character traits. Kenneth Wuest defines **agape** as *to value, consider precious, and hold in high regard*. This is God's position toward the entire human race.[3] Nevertheless, His Agape love has nothing to do with what we experience. Until God's love is believed and experienced, we can feel condemnation, rejection, and even hatred as if it's coming from God! In Colossians 1:21, Paul explained that because of our evil works, we consider ourselves to be enemies of God, but that only exists in OUR minds—not God's.

The Apostle John tells us the love of God is manifested in the propitiation, *"In this is love, not that we loved God, but that He loved us and sent His Son to be the propitiation for our sins."* (1 John 4:10) The word **propitiation** has a variety of meanings, but suffice it to say, in the propitiation for our sins, everything was satisfied that needs to be satisfied for us to enjoy absolute peace and harmony in our relationship with God.

The New Testament's expression of God's love can't be stated in one simple word; it's expressed with phrases like *perfect love* or *love completed*. The word **perfect** comes from a Greek word which means *to be complete, to finish, to carry something out, or to finish*. The idea of *complete* seems to indicate the completing of a goal or task; therefore, the Greek, which doesn't have the equivalent of the fourth Hebrew word Chaim mentioned, combines two words to convey the same idea.

The Bible makes a distinction between the love of God inherent in His character, motivating all His Words, commands and actions, and the love He seeks to share with His creation!

We were created in the likeness and image of God. As such, we can only enjoy life to its fullest when our core nature is love—not love as the world defines it, but love that holds God and others in high regard, considering them precious and valuable. This type of love is never selfish; it acts based on the value it holds for the object of its affection.

True Love doesn't waver in the face of personal flaws and repulsive behavior. It doesn't overlook the behavior or exempt them from accountability, but it still has value for the person.

When God's love accomplishes its intended purpose in our heart, we will trust Him. Faith works by love. When we believe God loves us, we're able to trust Him. When we trust Him, we put His Word into practice. As we experience the benefits of His wisdom, the quality of our life improves,

---

3   Kenneth Wuest, *Wuest's Word Studies from The Greek New Testament* (Grand Rapids: Eerdmans, 1968), p 60-61.

and we fall more deeply in love with Him. It's a never-ending cycle that leads to a deeper quality of love.

The Bible is very clear that the fruit of loving God is loving each other. John asks this sobering question, *"For he who does not love his brother whom he has seen, how can he love God whom he has not seen?"* (1 John 4:20) When we love (value) God, we love what He loves. When the goal of God's love reaches its completion, we love God, each other, and the world.

In all of this, however, we still haven't reached a clear definition of love, and what it looks like in application. Neither have we answered the question, "How do I know when I'm walking in love?"

It seems that in many circles of pop theology, the commandments and the love of God are mutually exclusive. This flawed theology arises from the Old Testament—New Testament dichotomy. One thousand eight hundred years of organized effort has accomplished its goal: seducing believers into thinking that the truth changed between the Covenants, implying God changed. The reality is, however, the truth never changed; the Covenants did.

Religion, since Mount Sinai to the 21st-century church, has made the commandments appear to be the unreasonable dictates of an oppressive God. In the commentary on the commandments in his book, *The Rational Bible,* Dennis Prager points out that eight of the Ten Commandments are instructions about how we should relate to one another. Only two are about how we should relate to God! All of the 613 commandments God gave were all based on the Ten. They were expanded to show how the Ten would be applied in a nation seeking civil order.

The commandments were given to show us how to walk in God's definition of love toward one another. They were meant to be self-governing prescriptions for how to have a great life with great relations. Instead, they became a standard for judging and controlling others.

The Apostle John said, *"By this we know that we love the children of God, when we love God and keep His commandments. For this is the love of God, that we keep His commandments."* (1 John 5:2-3)

Jesus said, *"If you love me, keep my commandments."* (John 14:15)

Love and the commandments are a paradox. The crooked heart sees them as religious works. The righteous heart sees them as prescriptions for expressing love contained within the heart. After all, love that's not expressed is of no value; it's nothing more than an emotion until it's expressed as a means of showing value for the recipient.

Rejection of the commandments as God's definition for expressing love is iniquity! Like all humanism, it makes man a god unto himself—determining good and evil independent of God and His truth!

In John chapters 14-15, Jesus explains a different kind of relationship that can be had by those who value and, therefore, attend to the commandments. Once again, the legalist sees this as earning benefits from God. The truth, however, is that these are people who trust God, honor His Word in the way they express love for each other and God. This trust and reverence are the basis for a reciprocal love relationship. God is treating you just as His commandments direct, and you're treating Him and others just as His commandments direct. This reciprocal relationship is love perfected… love as God intended!

You get to choose: Will you be content in the intellectual knowledge of God's love for but in the absence of a deeply intimate relationship? Or, will you choose to be that special one who holds nothing back and shares a heart-to-heart connection where you are His exclusively? Will you enter into that secret place where you share your every desire with Him and He shares His plans with you to help you map out your life? Will you allow Him to lead on this journey because you know His heart and genuinely trust Him for all things to work for your good? It's your choice! He's ready and waiting!

If you desire to explore the depths of God's incredible love, check out this audio series: Knowing and Feeling The Love of God (https://www.impactministries.com/product/knowing-and-feeling-the-love-of-god/).

WRATH

God said "fear not" more than any command in the Bible. He hasn't changed His mind!

Chapter 8

WRATH IS RARE

(Chaim Bentorah)

Zephaniah 1:18: *"Neither their silver nor their gold will be able to deliver them in the day of the Lord's wrath. But the whole land will be devoured by the fire of his jealousy."*

There was a large international engineering conference in France. During a break, one of the European engineers came into the room and announced: "Have you heard the latest dumb stunt by the United States? They sent an aircraft carrier to Indonesia to help the tsunami victims. What do they intend to do, bomb them?"

An American Boeing engineer stood up and calmly replied: "Our carriers have three hospitals on board that can treat several hundred people, they are nuclear powered and can supply emergency electrical power to shore facilities. They have three cafeterias with the capacity to feed 3,000 people three meals a day, they can produce several thousand gallons of fresh water from sea water each day, and they carry half a dozen helicopters for use in transporting victims and injured to and from their flight deck. We have eleven other such ships stationed throughout the world ready to offer similar humanitarian assistance.

A journalist reported the room got hushed.

Sure, the American military is trained for war, and at least some contingents of the military may be at war in the Middle East or some other troubled spot on the globe at any time. But how much do we hear about the other wars the American military fights, which represent a much bigger picture? They wage war against piracy, smuggling, drugs, and human trafficking. American hospital ships, in one year, have treated over a million non-military, non-Americans throughout the world. The American military has built schools, provided protection and security to the defenseless around the globe, and much more.

Humanitarian aid is a key component to the U.S. military. Never in the history of the world has a world-class military force devoted so much time and effort to humanitarian aid. Yet, few in the world, and even in this country, realize this. This is because America doesn't use it's military's humanitarian effort as propaganda. Few people in the world bother to look beyond the surface. They see a warship and a powerful military, not realizing that most of the American military is engaged in humanitarian pursuits.

I'm not saying this as a political statement or trying to wave the American flag (I realize many readers do not live the United States); these are just facts that I have found in my research. I never realized that the U.S. military engaged is so much humanitarian work.

My point in mentioning this is to illustrate how the Old Testament suffers a similar lack of understanding. Many people see the Old Testament as a book of God's wrath and anger. I have heard preachers condemn the Old Testament as a book filled with provincialism, elitism, tribalism, every nasty "ism" except communism. We all know who fathered that one.

Yet, God's love and mercy are mentioned much more than His wrath. Our surface understanding of the Old Testament leads us to see God as a warmonger killing innocent people by the thousands, just as the appearance of an American aircraft carrier strikes immediate thoughts of war and destruction in the mind of those who fail to see the truth beneath the surface.

Zephaniah 1:18 is an excellent example of reading a verse in the Old Testament and jumping to the conclusion that God is a God that will strike you down if you don't watch your step. *"Neither gold nor silver will deliver one from God's wrath."*

"Wrath." Oh, that sounds bad. But let's look at this word, "wrath." In Hebrew, it is *'Avar*. You can render *'Avar* as wrath if you wish, but our English word wrath has little to do with the Hebrew word. This is the same word used for passing over. Its Semitic origins come from a river that overflows its banks. It has the idea of going beyond one's borders. In other words, God's wrath is anytime He goes beyond the boundaries that He has set up for Himself. It doesn't have to mean anger or rage, as we think of as wrath. It could be that He is forced to do something He does not want to do.

I read where the average police officer will rarely pull his gun during his career. Rarer still will he actually fire his weapon at someone. Many police officers will go their entire career without firing their weapon at a suspect. If an officer does fire his weapon in the line of duty, that is *'Avar*; being forced to do something he does not want to do.

I'm not saying that the wrath of God does not encompass anger and fiery rage; you can believe that if you wish, it would not be an incorrect translation. I am saying that I find no rational reason to translate it this way. I prefer to translate *'Avar* as God acting like a police officer who is forced to use his gun; it goes beyond the way God normally deals with man

There are rare occasions when a police officer must resort to using his weapon to protect the innocent. We like to believe that when a police officer fires his weapon, it is not in anger or rage, he is only doing it to protect innocent life.

Can we not give God the same consideration?

To sign up for Chaim Bentorah's free daily Hebrew Word study, explore his books, and learn more about his in-depth biblical Hebrew online learning platform, please visit: https://www.chaimbentorah.com/

Chapter 9

HOW CAN A GOD OF LOVE HAVE WRATH

Excessive or extreme kindness to a perpetrator is injustice to the victim!

When love is defined by God's Word instead of by subjective humanism, it ventures past the boundaries of self-serving, iniquitous reasoning. God continuously expresses His passion for saving and protecting the innocent and those who can't protect themselves.

Humanism, socialism, and other carnal philosophies rally under the banner of human rights. Their claim for a morally superior life not only contradicts God's definitions of love but is self-contradicting and hypocritical. In practical application, we discover that these false concepts of love only show compassion for specific groups of people: the wicked, the murderers, and those who embrace their elitist ideology.

Mercy isn't overlooking fault or wrong-doing. **Mercy** is *continuing to be kind and respectful to those who don't deserve it*. For example, in America, all people are to be considered innocent until proven guilty. Even in the abundance of evidence, people are still allowed due process and to maintain their civil rights. By redefining mercy, we have a generation of believers who feel everyone should get by with almost anything; there should be no accountability and especially no punishment.

So, we ask, "Is it an act of kindness for the family of a murder victim for the perpetrator to receive a minimum sentence? Suppose an accountant embezzles the life savings of an elderly customer. Is it an act of kindness for that customer to suffer from poverty in the last years of life while the embezzler never repays a penny? No! We've reached a point of godlessness where good is called evil and evil is called good (Isa. 5:20-21).

Justice and mercy aren't values that can be applied independently. Without justice, lawlessness will rule. Without mercy, harsh legalism will rule. Either extreme will destroy civilization. God is both just and merciful. His wrath only overflows when doing so brings the proper balance of justice and mercy.

Workers of iniquity love to characterize Exodus 21:24's famously just phrase, *"An eye for an eye."* as a verse about vengeance. But it's actually a civil command that sustains justice and mercy. The goal isn't vengeance; it's protection for the innocent. God's justice demands that whatever you do, or attempt to do, to a person is what your penalty will be. In cases of theft, the thief should repay seven-fold. Even more incredible, it is the first civil code in the world that did not allow retaliation on entire families for the acts of one individual.

> This system of justice devalues the life of the innocent while exalting the life of the wicked.

If people can commit murder, knowing they may only do a few years in prison, they have no serious deterrent. This system of justice devalues the life of the innocent while exalting the life of the wicked. Suppose a single parent is killed and children are left without family or support. Generations of human lives can be destroyed due to the act of mercy given to the criminal.

Thieves steal because they don't want to work. If they have to repay their theft seven-fold, they may discover it's easier to work and earn money than to spend years working to repay their debt.

God's system of civil justice is designed, first and foremost, to protect the innocent, in two ways. First, the certainty of a penalty is the only effective deterrent to crime. The wicked don't curb their behavior in exchange for leniency. They consider you a "chump" when you make the way easy for them to commit more crime. Plus, there's no viable proof that leniency ever works to decrease crime. Second, justice occurs when there's an overflowing of wrath, as Chaim revealed, to protect the innocent.

In the face of justice, less crime is committed against the innocent. The foolish who are considering crime can observe and learn. If both mercy and justice are applied, offenders can be reformed and abandon their life of crime. Nevertheless, in all these scenarios, innocent people are protected!

According to Jesus, we are to *"Hang all the law and all the prophets on these two commandments: Love the Lord your God and love your neighbor as yourself."* (Matt. 22:37-40) From this and hundreds of other passages, we understand God's every Word and action is motivated by His value for mankind; therefore, every perceived brutal action we don't understand was also motivated by love and, in most cases, was intended to protect the innocent.

It seems that only Noah had a pure genealogy through which the Messiah could come, according to Genesis 6:9. At the time before The Flood, the earth was filled with wicked God-haters, Luciferians, and Nephilim who sought to annihilate that which God loved: the human race. Had God's passion for providing eternal life for His creation not "overflowed," Jesus couldn't have come, and the entire human race would have been eternally lost.

When Israel entered Canaan, they were in a "kill or be killed" situation with the pagan worshippers that inhabited the land. These countries were to be destroyed so as not to become thorns in their sides that deterred them from reaching the world with a demonstration of civil and social justice, revealing the loving nature of God as expressed through His commandments. Once again, God had to act to preserve the bloodline of the Messiah. Still today, the nations that continually attack Israel, seeking to destroy the world and ultimately ushering in the antichrist for worldwide persecution, will come from those nations God commanded them to destroy but didn't. As a result, millions of innocent believers are being tortured and even beheaded.

Nowhere else do we see God's love for mankind overflow than on the cross when it overflowed as wrath onto Jesus for our sins. Jesus became our sin, so we wouldn't have to live under the power of sin. He then bore God's wrath so we would never have to bear His wrath. *"With a little wrath I hid*

My face from you for a moment." (Isa. 54:8) God's wrath overflowed onto Him to protect us.

Many believers have redefined *wrath*, creating an unscriptural definition of the word. They need to make God fit into their humanistic paradigm. They cannot reconcile God's love and His wrath because of their humanistic definitions of love.

To the degree we minimize or redefine God's wrath, we minimize the price Jesus paid, thereby depreciating the immense, inimitable, unfathomable love God has for us. It was the Apostle John who emphasized the one place we can look at to grasp God's love being manifested: the propitiation—the price God paid because of His boundless value for you!

Would you consider apologizing to God for all the times you've blamed Him for what is in fact the consequences of our choices and actions? Will you repent (change your mind) and never again blame the consequences of your decisions and actions on God? Most importantly, will you listen when His still small voice says, "Don't walk down that path."?

The Covenant of Peace that ensures the believer will never experience God's wrath is the basis of the New Covenant. If this is an area where you desire to dive deeper into God's Word check out the book and audio series entitled The Gospel of Peace (https://www.impactministries.com/product/the-gospel-of-peace/).

CHASTISEMENT

The Father only teaches us as the favored child
of His love.

Chapter 10

LIKE THE TWINKLING OF AN EYE

(Chaim Bentorah)

Isaiah 51:4: *"I will make my judgment to rest for a light of the people."*

Yehudah ha-Levi, a medieval Jewish poet, displayed his emotion in a little rhyme: *Ein Rega' Beli Nega.* "There is no rest without a wound in it." The word rest in Hebrew is *Rega'* which is a very curious word in Hebrew. It means to be both at rest and to set in motion.

The first is more prevalent in Modern Hebrew as the expression *Bet Margo' a* which could mean a rest-home. Also, in Modern Hebrew, there is *Vulkan Reghe' a,* which would mean an anti-anxiety medication. A dormant volcano is a *Rak Rega'.* There is a simple exclamation in Modern Hebrew *Tiraago,* or relax.

Perhaps in Isaiah 51:4, we could best use the word, *moment*, rather than rest. *"I will make my judgment as a moment for a light of the people."* Linguists point out that the English word, moment, is derived from the word, *movement.* Its origins are in the hands of a clock, which help define a short time. In other words, this will take just a moment, or the time it takes for the hand of a clock to move. So too is the Hebrew word for motion or *Rega'.* The Hebrew word is pictured as the twinkling of an eye. The Septuagint uses the Greek word *Atomos* for *Rega',* which is the same Greek word that Paul used in I Corinthians 15:52 when referring to the coming of the Lord. Obviously, that is where we get our English word atom, referring to something tiny. To the Hebrews, *Rega'* is a motion so fast that you hardly notice the movement.

I read something interesting in the Talmud this morning. It asked the question: "How long indeed is a *Rega*? They answer *Rega' Ke-memreh* – as long as it takes to say *Rega'*.

In modern Israeli culture, I am told, *Rega'* is referred to as a silent gesture that involves bringing together the five fingertips of one hand and raising them – back of the hand facing the listener – at eye level. The listener understands that this gesture means *Rega'* – wait a minute. Such a gesture has been known to stop traffic in Israel. The rabbi who shared this with me does not recommend that gentiles or tourists, use it for this purpose.

So now we come back to Isaiah 54:4, where God says that He will make his judgment to *Rega'* for a light to His people. In the Hebrew, it is literally expressed *"My judgments, as a light to my people, will I make a rest."* The word light is *'or*, which is spelled *Aleph, Vav,* and *Resh.* The spiritual references to these letters are God, man, and the Holy Spirit. The Sages teach that the prime meaning of light, *'or*, is God's connection of man to His Spirit. The ancient teaching is that as we join or unite with God, God's light shines brighter. The closer we join ourselves with God, the brighter His light becomes. Unlike new-agers, who will say that we strengthen God and thus become little Gods ourselves, the sages are teaching that our joining with God is not increasing His power but increasing His joy and thus His joy becomes our strength. Hence Nehemiah 8:10, *"The joy of the Lord is our strength."*

God's judgments upon us are meant as a tool of correction, a chastisement (Hebrews 12), a demonstration of his love, to strip us of the sins that keep us from uniting with Him, so that His light or joy may fill us and thus increase our strength. But He is also promising that such judgment will be *Rega'* - for a moment, a twinkling of the eye. In the words of another Jewish expression, "This too will pass."

To sign up for Chaim Bentorah's free daily Hebrew Word study, explore his books, and learn more about his in-depth biblical Hebrew online learning platform, please visit: https://www.chaimbentorah.com/

Chapter 11

CHASTISEMENT BY GRACE

Grace teaches the lesson and gives you the power to learn and live it!

One term that has terrorized believers through the ages is **chastisement**. Religion has demonized God as a child abuser who beats, whips, sickens, maims, cripples, impoverishes, and even murders those we love as a means of teaching us a lesson. Maybe He was raised in a bad environment with poor communication skills. Not!

My longtime friend, Skip Adkins, whom I've known since I was fifteen, was extremely resistant to the gospel. So much so, he avoided me any time he could. He'd go so far as to run in a department store and hide behind a clothes rack if he saw me at the mall.

After eleven years of sharing the love of God with him, one early evening at my dinner table, he surrendered his life to Jesus. That was nearly forty years ago, and he's still walking with and serving God to this day! As we talked that night, after giving his life to the Lord, I asked why he'd been so resistant to the gospel. The details of his story were different than others, but it was the same issue I'd encountered most often: he was angry at God!

Skip was eleven years old when his father died. At the graveside, the preacher shook his hand and said, "Son, I don't know what God is trying to teach you." At that moment, his heart was obliterated, "What could I have possibly done that was so bad God would kill my father to teach me a lesson?"

Chastisement By Grace

You hear it every time a tornado rips through, destroying houses and taking lives. "I know God's in control and has a purpose for this." It's mind-boggling that no one has ever figured out the elusive message God's trying to send by all the devastation. Even more confusing is why God would do these heinous things to other people to teach us the lessons when they didn't do anything. Why not do them to those who need the lesson?

Jesus identified the thief—not God—as the one who comes to steal, kill, and destroy, juxtaposing Himself (by means of His sacrifice) as the giver of abundant life (John 10:10). Attributing the works of the devil to God is the epitome of calling good evil and evil good. God refers to them as the ones who take justice away from the righteous (innocent, Isa. 5:20-23).

The Scriptures very clearly illustrate *chastening* as the process for training a beloved or favored child, *"My son, do not despise the chastening of the Lord, nor detest His correction; for whom the Lord loves He corrects,* ***Just as a father the son in whom he delights."*** (Pro. 3:11-12) He doesn't chasten as a father who hates or despises his child.

The Father's chastening is motivated by love in this scripture. He has value for the child, considering the child precious, and holding that child in high regard. He'd do nothing to inflict self-hatred or low self-worth on this beloved son. Staying consistent with God's personal concept of love, He'd do it in a way that inspires reciprocal love, (value) for God, others, and self! God's not a hypocrite; He doesn't tell us to love and raise our children one way, only to do it Himself in the complete opposite way!

The distinction is clear that chastening is correction—not punishment. *Correction* is when we are redirected. I often think of the annoying voice on my GPS when I've missed my turn, "In one-quarter mile, make a legal U-turn." The recorded voice doesn't tell me I'm stupid for getting lost nor does the steering wheel pulsate with electrical shock waves up my arms. It simply provides instruction for a course correction so I can reach my desired destination on the quickest, easiest route.

Correction can, no doubt, be unpleasant. It's usually an affront to the ego. After all, we do what we do, the way we do it because we think it's the right way to get what we want. The pain we suffer from the path we've chosen isn't God's punishment for the wrong choice; it's the natural consequences of violating God's prescription for life, health, and happiness. The pain of correction is dying to *self*, i.e., our vain attempts to have the life we desire independent of God!

As the gospel spread into pagan, Gentile cultures, those groups tended to interpret the Gospel in light of their previously held, pagan beliefs. **Asceticism** was one of the many popular beliefs that had an early influence on Christian-religious thought. This occult belief was based on self-denial (purity through suffering).

The Catholic Church didn't really preach the gospel. No doubt they embraced some aspects of the teaching of Jesus, but its doctrines were more pagan-based than biblical. They overwhelmingly rejected Jesus' and the apostles' teaching of salvation by faith. They taught a version of Jesus and His mission on earth that wasn't in the Scripture. In fact, it was through the church's deliberate efforts that the concept of an outdated, no longer relevant Old Testament was developed, paving the way for it pagan roots to explain the work of Jesus on the cross.

The rejection of salvation by faith closed the door to Jesus as our righteousness. As such, **repentance** was replaced by *penance*: *self-inflicted punishment for sin*, diminishing the suffering of Christ on the cross as nothing more than an example of suffering and not the ultimate venue for reconciliation through propitiation. The problem with salvation by works begs the question, "How many good works must we do to be saved, and who gets to be the one to define that?"

In pagan-based religion, we must suffer to become purified (made righteous) if we want to go to heaven. Of course, the length of time and the degree of suffering would be determined by the church. This suffering would include but wasn't limited to self-mutilation, humiliating public acts, and substantial financial donations to the church. Eventually, it evolved into advancing payments on sin, otherwise known as *indulgence*. Indulgence was the way the wealthy avoided penance! Many wealthy political leaders would pay an indulgence to keep a mistress on the side and still go to heaven.

Our modern concept of *chastisement* evolved from this warped ideology. According to Arch Bishop Trench, Augustine purposely redefined this word[4] that once reflected God lovingly redirecting His children for their

---

4 Richard Chenevis Trench, *Synonyms of the New Testament*,

benefit, to tormenting them as a means of making them pay for their sins.

Unbeknownst to many believers, God is always consistent. His Word never contradicts itself. Correction is designed to get a person back on course; therefore, it's designed to bring about repentance. In Romans 2:4, Paul points out that, *"The goodness of God draws us to repentance."* a goodness and patience despised by many to this very day. Brutality may bring about a change of behavior, but only mercy and truth touch the heart to bring us to repentance. Psalm 25:10 tells us, *"All the paths of the Lord are mercy and truth."*

The church majority has rejected the holiness of God outright by insisting that He's common, like the pagan gods they worshipped who brought pain and suffering to force their followers into submission. God, being holy (uncommon), treated us as children, not as slaves, but as a loving father treats his beloved children. He sought to teach and develop us. He never hid His wise ways from us; He wants us to be as wise, compassionate, and trusting as He is. Those who don't understand God's ways are those who refuse to be taught by His Word!

Because of the New Covenant, we can experience what no believer ever consistently experienced before the resurrection: the grace of God! Sadly, the definition of **grace** has been limited to merely *unmerited favor*. While it's true, it's only a partial definition. The Greek word for *grace* is *charis,* the root word for *charismata* which is interpreted as *gifts*—as in gifts of the Holy Spirit; therefore, *grace* is when *a power works in us and manifests the true character and nature of God*!

Under the New Covenant, we're immersed into Christ, and He's immersed into us. When we believe this, we have the opportunity to be one with Him and share in all He is and all He can do: *charismata*. Grace is undeniably divine favor, kindness, and graciousness, but it's also a capacity and ability that works from the heart. Grace is the power of God that works in us as we yield our hearts to Him to do and be all He says we can do and be: a manifestation of the life of Christ in and through us!

Titus 2:11-12 presents an overlooked aspect of God grace.

> *For the grace of God that brings salvation has appeared to all men,* **teaching us** *that,* **denying ungodliness** *and* **worldly lusts**, *we should* **live soberly, righteously,** *and* **godly** *in the present age.*

(Grand Rapids: Baker Book House, 1989) p125.

The same grace that brings salvation also teaches us, in the same way a loving father teaches a beloved child; thus, in the New Covenant, grace not only gives us the capacity to learn but is the transformative power to grow into the truth we learn. In *Disciplined By Grace,* J.F. Strombeck says, "All impartation of spiritual truth, all instruction, all reproof, all admonition, all exhortation, and all chastening are elements of the discipline of grace."[5]

The New Covenant reality is that the Holy Spirit chastens us by revealing that we're the righteousness of God in Christ (2 Cor. 5:21). With Christ in us, we have the capacity and ability to overcome sin. We have no excuse or justification for failure other than unbelief. God's always reminding us we can... if we're willing!

In the New Testament, the word usually translated as **tempted** or **tried** actually means *to test, try, scrutinize, tempt to evil and to make to strive.* This is the same definition Augustine gave to the word *chasten.* It was James, however, who said:

> *Let no man say when he is tempted (tested, tried, scrutinized or made to strain), 'I am tempted (tested, tried, scrutinized and made to strain) by God'; for God cannot be tempted with evil, neither does He tempt (test, try, scrutinize and make to strive) any man.* (Jam. 1:13)

Isaiah 53 details how Jesus became our sin, carried all the consequences for our sin, and was chastened by God so that we could have peace.

We can accept the words of religious paganism and suffer from fear and condemnation, or we can accept the finished work of Jesus on the cross and flourish in love and peace. When you begin to feel condemned about your actions, consider admitting to yourself and God that you know you made a mistake. Then turn to God and ask Him for the wisdom you need to make godly choices. Then, remind yourself, "Because of Jesus, I'm forgiven. God isn't seeking to punish me but to teach me. Jesus was chastised in my place so I could have peace. Father, I accept your peace even though it's not what I deserve, and I open my heart to learn from you."

Check out www.impactministries.com for hundreds of free in depth videos that will establish you in the immovable, unchangeable love of God.

---

5   J.F. Strombeck, *Disciplined by Grace,* (Grand Rapids: Kregel, 1991) p.11

CURSE

God draws us to repentance by His goodness. A curse has no redemptive quality!

Chapter 12

CURSED IN OUR OWN STRENGTH

(Chaim Bentorah)

Jeremiah 17:5: *"Thus saith the Lord; 'Cursed be the man that trusteth in man, and maketh flesh his arm whose heart, departeth from the Lord."*

Curse – Hebrew: *'Arur* – Curse, to remove the influence of God.

Thank goodness this verse was written in Hebrew and not English. Just because some English-speaking lexicographer decided that *'Arur* means curse in English, everyone jumps on the bandwagon declares that God curses or invokes evil on people according to our English definition of the word, curse.

Curse in Hebrew is *'Arur*, which comes from the idea of a situation where God is not present. To curse someone is to demand that God removes His protective covering, His *Succoth*, or arm of protection, from that person.

In Jeremiah 17:5, the word *'Arur* is passive. Hence, this is not an act of God, but a result of what will happen if we trust in the arm of the flesh. An example of this is found in Isaiah 38. The Babylonians are at Judah's doorstep hungry for God Jehovah. What does Hezekiah do with these potential converts? He begins to show off his wealth and power.

Let me digress. In Isaiah 38, we learn Hezekiah is about to die. God grants him fifteen more years of life, and as a sign, He holds back 40 minutes on Ahaz's sundial. Hezekiah was not the only one to marvel at this sign. The Babylonians were devoted stargazers, and when signs in the skies got a little messed up due to God's holding back the sun, the Babylonians figured that this is a God they needed to help them in their fight against the Assyrians.

Think about it. God performs this great miracle, grants Hezekiah an extended life and even allows him to team up with a mega-nation and make a name for God. What does Hezekiah do? He shows off what a powerful and anointed king he thinks he is. Hezekiah was trusting in the *"arm of the flesh,"* and we learn in Jeremiah 17:5 that God will curse such a person.

"Arm of the flesh" is *Zera'o* (arm, strength) *Basar* (flesh, human initiative). This means to plant or conceive in the flesh; to depend on the strength of human initiative.

God uses secular work, human skills, and human knowledge. He uses physicians, lawyers, politicians, etc. But we can't look to *"the arm of the flesh"* to pull us through. Our *Zera'o* (arm, strength)" is in Jehovah, not in *Basar* (flesh, human initiative). If we trust in our own strength, our (*Zera'o*) lies in the flesh (*Basar*). By removing God as our strength we have effectively cursed ourselves.

How often do we venture out in our own strength and think nothing of it, little realizing that we are cursed by going this venture without God?

To sign up for Chaim Bentorah's free daily Hebrew Word study, explore his books, and learn more about his in-depth biblical Hebrew online learning platform, please visit: https://www.chaimbentorah.com/

Chapter 13

THE CURSE WITHOUT CAUSE DOES NOT COME

The curse is getting what you want, and then living with the consequences!

The concept of a *curse* can be challenging to understand in any language because it can have many different meanings based on a number of variables. Proverbs 26:2 has this to say about a curse, *"the curse causeless shall not come."* Who or what, then, causes the curse and why?

As is typical with religion, everything negative is blamed on God; He either does it or allowed it. The positive events that happen in our lives are often considered to be good luck or even sometimes attributed to the devil! Regardless of who is blamed, the one individual that never seems to bear any responsibility is the individual upon whom the curse comes.

Sin has many subtle components, but we know this: all aspects of sin lead to death. The fullness of death isn't immediately manifested, but death is set into motion the moment sin is conceived in our heart. Religion only acknowledges sin after it's put into practice, reducing it to a behavioral problem. Sin, however, is a process that begins in the thoughts and intentions of the heart where, like all types of faith, whether for good or evil, are conceived! It's the intentions of our hearts that embolden us to take the next step toward application. Behavior is simply another manifestation in the continuum of sin and death! So, let's be sure we understand what sin is.

While there have been many valid studies written about sin, there seems to be one key missing component to our definition of sin, which is neither understood nor discussed. The accepted definition of **sin** is to *miss the mark or fall short*. Sin, however, isn't simply falling short; it's *falling short of or missing the* **glory of God**. It's not just missing the mark; it's *missing the mark of the high calling*. Understanding the seductive nature and power of sin to bring death is only grasped when we understand this: it's not what we do wrong that destroys us as much as it's what we miss out on!

Darkness is the absence of light; however, light isn't the absence of darkness. Light always overcomes darkness. The destructive power of sin is rooted in its ability to pervert the way we perceive God. It's entering into darkness; therefore, it perverts and diminishes the way we see and perceive both God and ourselves. Failure to see God as He is gives rise to every false religion, the world's system, all unbelief, and every struggle with the flesh.

> All human beings have physical desires; they aren't wrong or evil, they're natural.

All human beings have physical desires; they aren't wrong or evil… they're natural. Desires can endear us to God or drag us away from God. What makes them good or evil is how we fulfill them. Sexual desire can be fulfilled in a godly relationship that bonds two people together in love, who give glory to God for the intimacy they share, or … it can be fulfilled by cheating.

2 Peter 1:4 tells us we have exceedingly great and precious promises in Jesus. He then makes a statement that's constantly overlooked *"Through these you may be partakers of the divine nature, having escaped the corruption that is in the world through lust."* When we trust God is good—and only good—we have the assurance that He desires to fulfill our every desire in a way that keeps us in harmony with Him!

So, what is the curse? If we remove our religious glasses, we realize the **curse** is *the natural consequence of sin*. In other words, it's when we get what we want, even though God has warned us of the consequences.

As mentioned previously, the law of the seed is the underpinning law of all things that exist in our universe. The first principle of the **law of the seed** is this: *every seed bears fruit after its own kind*. God doesn't make an individual decision over every seed planted as to whether or not it will grow and bear fruit. He doesn't individually decide what kind of fruit a seed will produce. The fruit is the product of the natural law.

Adam was warned not to eat of the tree of knowledge of good and evil. He was told it would produce the fruit of death. He wasn't told God would kill him. He was told it would be the natural consequences of the knowledge of good and evil—independent of God—that would kill him.

At some point, Adam chose not to believe he was already like God, which means he didn't believe it when God told him he had authority over the earth (Gen. 1:27-28). He didn't realize the magnitude that, being the only humans alive, their total ruling authority in Planet Earth would bring about a worldwide change once he and Eve became flesh. God didn't curse Adam neither did He curse the earth. Adam's curse was simply this: he got what he wanted, thereby becoming a god unto himself. Likewise, God didn't curse the earth. He warned Adam the natural results of his choice(s) and the effects it would have, *"Cursed is the ground because of you."* (Gen. 3:17)

After becoming flesh, Adam was no longer a living soul, i.e., a soul dominated by the quality of life God possessed. When he became his own god, he was dominated by the quality of life he could create. In this, man got what he wanted... but at the cost God warned. Adam and Eve didn't fall over dead the moment they partook of the fruit. It was what was conceived in their heart that caused death to begin to consume them. They began to die the moment they conceived of their reasoning in their heart.

Many different words are translated as *curse* with subtle differences in meaning. Regardless of their meaning, the intention of God never changes. Humans live in the consequences of their choices despite the fact that God always desires and endeavors to bring about a relationship. God will not and cannot violate the free will He gave to mankind.

We often see phrases like *"I will cause..."* In the English translation, it sounds as if God is actually causing the consequences. In the Hebrew, that's not always the case. God is the creator of all things. In western thought, there's little realization of the necessity for polar opposites; nevertheless, all reality has a polar opposite. These opposites aren't antagonistic; they are, in fact, complimentary. Night and day aren't in a battle for supremacy; they're harmonious. They're both required for life on our planet. There can't be good without evil. There can't be energy without rest. There can't be hot without cold. If God creates a path that leads to Him, then choosing to walk in the opposite direction is to be moving away from Him.

God designed the law of gravity to work for our good. However, like all polar opposites, we can use it for life or death. It keeps us alive by holding us to the planet. Its downward force actually contributes to our bone density. Despite the long list of positive ways gravity affects us, if we jump off the roof of a house, we risk harm and possible death.

When translating this concept from Hebrew to English, it would probably sound like this, "If you jump off the house, I will it to bring suffering." The question is this, "Does God decide if we suffer, and, if so, how does He decide the degree of suffering? If not, why would He say He will cause it?" Since God created the law of gravity, He has indirectly caused the harm. God attempts to warn us of the dangers of misusing His prescriptions (commands). We can make them work for us or we can make them work against us.

Before assuming that I'm grasping at straws, consider an insightful teaching about how the heart works. The parable of the sower is the key parable to understanding how the believer experiences the kingdom of heaven, i.e., heaven on earth.[6] Jesus uses this parable to explain the universal law of the seed (AKA the law of sowing and reaping) from a heart perspective.

In the illustration about law of the seed, the heart is the soil. It's the soil that produces the crop based on the type of seed we plant, i.e., what we hear and think, and the degree to which we nurture it in our thoughts, imagination, and meditation. Then, Jesus says, *"For whoever has, to him more will be given; but whoever does not have, even what he has will be taken away from him."* (Mark 4:25)

It sounds (and interpreted) as if someone outside of us will give more or take away what we have, namely... God. By considering context in the preceding verse, *"With the same measure you use, it will be measured to you."* and study the original language, *"giving and taking away"* is the product of our heart, the types of seeds we have planted, and the degree of thought, imagination, and meditation we have given to those seeds (nurturing).

When we plant the seed of God's promises, we grow a crop of fulfilled

---

6   Jim Richards, *Heaven on Earth,* (Traveler's Rest: True Potential, 2019).

spiritual promises. But when we are in lack, our every thought and imagination about lack plants thorns that grow up and choke out the seeds of promise, which means we lose even the good that we have.

We experience the curse because we fill our heart with seeds of sin, low self-worth, feelings of lack, and unbelief that can only produce more of itself. By what we hear, think, ponder, and consider, we fill our hearts with thorns leaving no room for any of the goodness of God. We alienate ourselves from the life God has freely given (Eph. 4:18). This is the curse!

The Apostle Paul provided the two cornerstone scriptures for living a great life, *"For all the promises of God in Him are Yes, and in Him Amen, to the glory of God through us."* (2 Cor. 1:20) and *"Christ has redeemed us from the curse of the law, having become a curse for us."* (Gal. 3:13) Once again, we find ourselves challenged to either see God as He revealed Himself through Jesus at the cross or through the eyes of religion.

"As the bird by wandering, as the swallow by flying, so the curse causeless shall not come. A whip for the horse, a bridle for the ass, and a rod for the fool's back". (Pro. 26:2-3) In this scripture lies both insight and hope. Curses don't just randomly happen. As we now know, a curse is the result of pursuing what we want in a way that promotes death and in the very same way God warns us not to pursue it.

So, where is the hope? Fools are people who refuse to learn from instruction. They don't trust God and, most likely, don't trust their parents or others who could help them. The outlook for fools seems hopeless, and, yet, one last opportunity remains. The context of the curse is understood by both good and bad consequences. Verse three isn't suggesting we beat everyone who isn't teachable. The whip or bridle prods the stubborn animal to follow directions. Facing the consequences of our actions can often be the whip or bridle, which has the potential to make us realize we'd do better following God's directions instead. In others words, God hasn't abandoned us to the curse we brought upon ourselves. When we won't learn by instruction, maybe we'll open our eyes when we experience the consequences.

> Fools are people who refuse to learn from instruction.

Remember, when you're suffering from the consequences of your actions, it's only because you were too foolish to listen when God tried to warn you. He doesn't want you living in the curse of your own making. There will always be those who are too stubborn and selfish to learn from their consequences. The most dangerous fool of all, though, is the religious fool who not only deceives himself but anyone who will listen as He blames God.

A tremendously beneficial study for overcoming foolishness is to read a chapter of Proverbs every day. I recommend using the Amplified Bible which is easily accessible through a variety of free mobile apps or downloadable versions online. Every time you see the words *fool* or *foolish,* write out that scripture and consider if it describes any aspect of how you manage your life, make decisions, or are currently experiencing those consequences. Repent of those tendencies and decide what biblical character trait you desire to put on to replace those that are creating your problems.

The story of Job has been twisted by religion to make us believe God uses torment and suffering as a teaching tool. What religion doesn't tell you is this: Job was rebuked for saying *"The Lord giveth and the Lord taketh away."* In fact, every negative thing Job said about why he was suffering was proven incorrect when God began to speak. Discover what Job learned when, instead of believing what he had heard about God, he actually saw him for himself. Check out this audio series: The Truth About Job (https://www.impactministries.com/product/why-do-bad-things-happen-to-good-people-the-truth-about-job/).

CONNECTION

In one intimate connection, God imparts more than we can learn from all the books in the world.

Chapter 14

GOD WANTS TO GIVE YOU A KISS

(Chaim Bentorah)

Numbers 12:8 *"With him (Moses) I will speak mouth to mouth, manifestly and not in dark places and the similitude of the Lord does he behold."*

Aaron and Miriam, Moses' brother and sister, began to have some doubts about Moses' leadership. Moses had married an Ethiopian woman, and they began to question if Moses was fit for his leadership role because of this marriage. Miriam even suggested that God spoke to her and Aaron just as much as He did to Moses, so what made Moses so special. God stepped in and set the record straight.

God advised Aaron and Miriam that when he speaks through a prophet, it is through dreams and visions, but with Moses, it is *"Mouth to mouth, manifestly and not in dark places and the similitude of the Lord does he behold."*

The word used in the Hebrew for *mouth* is *Peh*. This happens to be the same root as the letter *Pei Peh* means *mouth* or an *opening or entrance*. *Peh* is also cognate to the word *Poh*. This means *here* or *in this place*. Actually, when you compare the use of the word *Poh* you find it is used to describe a very special place, a place *where things very important happen*. Note too, the phrase is *peh el peh' adevar bo*. Literally, this is translated: *mouth to mouth in him*. The use of the preposition *Beth* or *in* gives us a little hint of something more profound. It indicates the touching of these mouths.

Other uses of the word *Peh* is an *entrance way, opening, or border*. The mouth and the nostrils are the only entrances into the inner man. God went further to say that He spoke plainly to Moses, not in *dark places*. The word in Hebrew for *dark places* is *Chidoth*, which is an *enigma* or *mystery*. He does speak to his prophets in visions and dreams, but these are often shrouded in mysteries and are not clear. With Moses, he spoke *clearly* and *plainly*, there was no second guessing. As dreams and visions are open to individual interpretation, what God had to say to Moses was plain enough, no interpretation was needed.

Then God adds: *"The similitude of the Lord does he behold."* Similitude in Hebrew is *Temenu*, which has the idea of *likeness*. Moses would take on the *likeness of God* in the conversation. This would be *likeness in desires and wishes*. He could only accomplish this by knowing God's heart.

Here's the interesting thing of what God is telling Aaron and Miriam. God gives a prophet a vision or a dream, which the prophet will interpret. However, there is a difference in His relationship with Moses. With Moses, it is not God speaking to Him, but it is *mouth to mouth*, God and Moses speaking to *each other*. Then there is the preposition, *in. Mouth to mouth in him*. Taking *mouth* as an *entrance or opening*, this is coming out as a picture of God speaking to the heart of Moses by pressing his mouth against the mouth of Moses.

What Christian has not said, *"God spoke to my heart."*? That seems to carry more weight than God speaking in visions or mysteries. What puts this exchange on a higher level than a dream or vision is that it is not only *God speaking to the heart of Moses*, it is *Moses speaking to the heart of God*. You see, *mouth to mouth* is an ancient Semitic expression of the communication through a kiss. An expression of intimacy.

God can reveal things to us in visions and dreams, but they are not always clear. He can reveal things in circumstances, coincidences, etc. We tend to guess that it is of God, or God speaking, but we are never really that clear about it. However, if like Moses, we speak heart to heart with God and if we know God's heart, then what He speaks will be very plain and clear. In other words, if we allow God to *kiss us*, words need not be exchanged.

In this modern Western culture, that image can creep some of us out, especially if we are men. But remember, God has no gender. The Semitic people had no problem with men *kissing* each other without a sexual connotation. They did not kiss on the lips; usually, it was the cheek or forehead. Still, they had no problem with the idea of *kissing God or God kissing them.* We in the Western culture do. We cannot imagine such intimacy with God, so we simply say God speaks to us *mouth to mouth* or *heart to heart.* For us, that seems a little less creepy.

A common question for many Christians, especially new Christians, is, "How do you know that God is speaking to you?" How do you hear God's voice? Moses gives us the answer; we will know God's voice when we know His heart. A woman will not kiss her husband or boyfriend on the mouth unless she is sure he understands her heart. A kiss is a physical expression of the heart. In a kiss, one's heart does all the talking.

The ancients believed that shepherds conversed with their sheep. Not with words, but with their hearts. And the sheep knew their shepherd's heart and responded. Perhaps that is what Jesus had in mind when he said in John 10:27, *"My sheep hear my voice, and I know them and they follow me."*

In Aramaic, the word for voice is *Qala,* which could mean an inner voice or the voice of the heart. It comes from a Semitic root word, *QL,* which means "key." The word for hear, in Aramaic, is *shema,* which is an *understanding.* The word for know, is *yida,* which is an *intimate knowing.* It is a word often used to describe the intimacy between a man and a woman.

In a sense, Jesus was saying, *"My sheep understand my heart and as a result, I am intimate with them and they follow me."* Jesus wants to communicate with us as God did with Moses, *mouth to mouth,* or *heart to heart.*

A man and woman who deeply love each other sometimes do not need to speak, they can hold each other and look into each other's eyes and their hearts will speak more than words. When a man and woman kiss, they are not speaking with their mouths, but in that kiss, their hearts are speaking volumes to each other. So too, when God holds us, and we allow Him to kiss us, mouth to mouth. We do not need to say a word, for our hearts are doing all the talking, and we will naturally follow all of His heart's desires.

To sign up for Chaim Bentorah's free daily Hebrew Word study, explore his books, and learn more about his in-depth biblical Hebrew online learning platform, please visit: https://www.chaimbentorah.com/

Chapter 15

THE MYSTERY OF TRANSFORMATION

As effortless as light illuminating the dark, so is transformation in the presence of God!

Transformation isn't becoming something you're not; it's becoming who you really are. Transformation isn't the result of gathering more intellectual information; it's a supernatural experience whereby God's reality becomes ours. I'm not saying it becomes our intellectual reality. I'm saying that we experience a new reality that alters our entire being from the inside out!

As Chaim points out, God communicated with Moses *"mouth-to-mouth."* Essentially, He "kissed him on the lips." For some, that may seem like a strange way to transmit information, and that would be right! The goal in God's interaction with us, however, isn't to transmit information—it's to transmit life! The exchange of life can be known but never explained; it can be experienced but never taught.

My wife and I've been married and passionately in love for nearly forty years. Most of those years, I've worked from my study in our home. Yes, we're in the same house 24 hours per day. Throughout the day, she may come into my study, kiss me, hold me for a few seconds, and walk out the door. Likewise, I do the same to her.

When we hold one another and kiss, we don't spend an inordinate amount of time explaining why we kissed or what we felt or meant by it. Actually, talking would cheapen the moment. When two people who are deeply in love (fully trusting in one another and committed to the best for one another) share a kiss, there's an instant download of information and a resultant experience. While the experience brings the realization of the information, the information can never bring a realization of the experience. In fact, the moment it was explained, we'd make a judgment about what the experience should be or mean instead of allowing it to be what it is.

In studying the Hebrew word for **life**, I reached what I think is a phenomenal conclusion. When Adam and Eve partook of the fruit from the Tree of Life, they had an experience that could only be understood by those having the same experience. Conversely, after eating from the fruit of the Tree of the Knowledge of Good and Evil, they wanted an explanation for understanding the life of God to facilitate what they intellectually determined the experience should be.

Unfortunately, as humans, we rarely speak the same love language as God. He speaks a life experience that manifests through transformation. We speak information designed to produce understanding.

The Bible speaks of **reconciliation** in Jesus. This word means *exchange*. God desires that we commune with Him through Jesus—like the kiss on Moses' lips, thereby experiencing an exchange. But what is it that's exchanged? We experience the love of God through the resurrection life, intimate connection, validation, and feelings of safety, peace, and acceptance. There are no adequate words to describe the exchange, and there are no human experiences with which to compare the exchange. There's just no way to explain the Creator of the universe's otherworldly expression of love!

> Westerners look for every excuse to reject a Creator God but have readily substituted religious Gnosticism with science.

Westerners look for every excuse to reject a Creator God but have readily substituted religious Gnosticism with science. While it's not called a religion, it meets all the criteria. Like the ancients, we believe we can control the "natural powers" with enough knowledge—the same pursuit of the occult for thousands of years.

The truth is, God is the only source for understanding why anything exists. Likewise, God is the only source to know the "how" of the beginning of any process in the universe. Science doesn't know the "why" or "how" of anything; yet, we observe and discover "how" and assume that makes us masters of the known world, but it makes us masters of nothing. We somehow convince ourselves that knowing the information makes us superior.

One of the most significant challenges of the human race is to resist being gods unto ourselves by vainly and egotistically thinking information is a substitute for experience. Even more devastating for the believer is trying to trust that information alone can bring about transformation. Accurate information is absolutely essential, but it's only part of the sequence that leads us to personal experience.

After working in the health field for nearly thirty years, I realized this phenomenon wasn't limited to the mind-set of believers. The entire human race has the capacity to know good and evil; therefore, we seek to gather knowledge under the assumption that, with enough knowledge, we can change anything… anything but ourselves, that is. Despite all of our issues, at our core, we don't want to change; we want everyone and everything else to change.

In our heart-to-heart connection to God, we experience Him. His light drives out our darkness and BOOM—unexplainable transformation occurs! Once we have His light, we can perceive and understand what we previously could not! How did we get so far from the relational, experiential core of knowing God?

When the Bible was translated into English, centuries of legalistic dogma had already been established. The translators had little, if any, knowledge of Hebrew history and culture from which to understand biblical terminology. Plus, the church was an organized power structure designed to convey absolute power onto the heads of state and the ultimate power onto the head of the church.

In those times, dissenters could be imprisoned, flogged, tortured, or burned at the stake on what were minor doctrinal differences. The issue wasn't the doctrinal ideology; it was the need for the church to have absolute control. On a side note, those who most harshly condemned the church for its closed-minded brutality and resistance to open discussions are the same people who support those same agendas in government today!

The English Bible is full of deliberate attempts to change the meanings of passages, as well as obscure the meanings of many words. Some words weren't translated; they were transliterated—the phonic spelling of words from one language to another instead of translating them. Why? Proper translations would have put the translators in opposition to the official position of the church. Similarly, words not in the original text were added for the same reasons.

None of the intentional or accidental mistranslations are bad enough to destroy an individual's faith… unless an unrepentant (unteachable) heart prefers its beliefs over God's Word. Since His Word and His intentions are already written in the deep recesses of our heart, we experience an inner witness of harmony when we renew our mind with His Word. That inner witness is a "knowing" that involves spirit and soul; we become sure with all of our being. At this stage, however, it's still just information.

Make no mistake, renewing the mind is the precursor to transformation, but it's not a substitute. New information stimulates the ego, giving the sensation that we've changed, grown… even won the battle. The momentary rush of ego disappears when, in real life, we discover all the same problems still exist. Since the mind seeks to protect the ego, we think that we just need more information. An endless cycle ensues in a foolish attempt to replace revelation with information and transformation with ego. When the goal is transformation, we will utilize the information to renew our mind, bringing it in harmony with God's Word.

Think of renewing the mind like a runway. The runway is essential to flight, but it's not flight. The runway is the precursor, not the substitute. It's essential for the plane to reach a specific ground speed proportional to its weight to ensure lift. That's the purpose of the runway. Flight, however, doesn't occur until there is lift-off.

Renewing the mind is like our runway. Based on the weight of our past, certain information is critical for reaching the proper speed to achieve lift-off (transformation). There's no separating the runway from liftoff, but without it regardless of how close to airspeed one travels, there is no flight. Likewise, irrespective of how much information we gather, it doesn't equal transformation.

Renewing the mind is reading God's Word, a picture of reality but not reality itself. The written Word of God is a verbal account of that which can never be fully explained. It's put into words that people interpret based on their predetermined beliefs, which is described in the Bible as looking *"through a glass darkly"* (1 Cor. 13:12). If the picture we create is desirable enough, we're inspired to have a look for ourselves. Then, like Job, we move from hearing about God to seeing and experiencing Him for ourselves.

A humble heart will surrender personal preferences and opinions to God's view and opinion. It will abandon a reality limited to our own experience for God's reality, which will bring an entirely different experience.

In Philippians 3:10, Paul talks of knowing *"The fellowship of His sufferings."* Refusing to believe God's account of the exchange that took place on the cross minimizes Jesus' sufferings to the level we deem acceptable to suffering ourselves. By rejecting the work of the cross that delivers us from suffering from our sins, we choose to suffer instead.

The word ***fellowship*** is a unique word. We've reduced and redefined it to something like "hanging out to chit-chat about spiritual things or sharing a meal." This word is actually a faith-based, meditative process wherein we share in something someone else owns.[7]

When we consider, reflect on, and imagine the information we've learned about the death, burial, and resurrection, to the point it becomes alive in our heart, we've participated in the biblical process of meditation. Philemon 6 describes it this way, *"That the communication of thy faith may become effectual by the acknowledging of every good thing which is in you in Christ Jesus."*

The word ***communication*** is from the Greek word *koinonia*, which means *fellowship*. ***Effectual*** can mean *effective or activated*. ***Acknowledging*** is from the Greek word *gnosis* which means *to experience fully*. This scripture should read more like, *"The sharing in what you have in common with Jesus, through your faith, activates your experience of every good thing which is in you in Christ Jesus."*

When our heart harmonizes with God's Word and then experiences it as an inner reality, we reach the end of the runway and take flight into an experience called transformation. Our transformation doesn't merely bring

---

7   Biblesoft, Inc., *Thayer's Greek Lexicon*, (Online: Biblesoft, 2006).

about a paradigm shift; it brings about a shift in our experiential reality!

Take a few minutes to do an exercise in communing with Christ. Start by closing your eyes and imagining Jesus on the cross. Try to see and experience every detail you can. Then, acknowledge to Him, "I choose to die with you." Create an image that represents all your sin, sickness, and circumstances going into Him, until you see yourself completely drawn into Him. Then, see yourself die and bound in Hades with Him. Now, the most important part, see Him come up out of the grave and ascend to the right hand of the Father. See yourself being raised with Him and seated at the right hand of God. Once again, acknowledge, "I am in you. I died with you. I'm raised up with you in newness of life, and I'm seated at the right hand of God with you." Allow yourself to abide in that moment for as long as you desire, experiencing resurrection life.

You can become anyone the Bible says you can be. If you want to be a peacemaker, an encourager, or simply a vessel of honor you must make the choice and God will provide the power. To get a great tool to guide you through the process as a gift from me, please visit: https://www.impact-ministries.com/ for *The Emotional Character Sketch* to help you with your journey from foolishness to wisdom!

JUDGMENT

Every decision is a judgment that works for us or against us; there is no third option!

Chapter 16

EVERY ACT BRINGS ITSELF INTO JUDGMENT

(Chaim Bentorah)

Ecclesiastes 12:14: *"Because God will bring every act to judgment, everything which is hidden, whether it is good or evil."*

It is interesting that the word for God has a definite article in front of it, "Because *The God*." The word for God is *Haelohim*, which is referring to one who has authority over us. The root word is *Alah*, the same as in the Arabic. In one respect, Muslims do worship the same God we do. When they talk of Allah, they are referring to the God of Abraham, Isaac, and Jacob. Their spin on God, however, is quite different than ours.

Elohim has a broad range of meaning. It is used to refer to God Jehovah, to angels and even to human judges. In this case, the definite article is used to express the fact that there may be many gods out there that people serve, but there is only One who will call our actions into judgment, that is "The God."

He will call all our *acts* or *Asah* into judgment. *Asah* means works, produce, and creations. *Asah* refers not only to physical acts but spiritual acts. This includes the creations of our imaginations. One aspect of this judgment is whether the creations of our imaginations are *good* or *Tov*, i.e., in harmony with God or *evil* (Hebrew –*Ra*). This particular *Ra* word has a reference to evil intentions. It is to be envious, hurtful to others. It has its origins in the mind. Hence these acts that God will call into judgment are not just outward acts, but actions that take place in the mind. Do our imaginations create things that are in harmony with God, or do they have evil intentions?

Note that both will be called into *judgment.* This idea of *bringing* into judgment uses the word *Yavi* for *brings.* This is in a hiphil imperfect form. Hence, every act will cause itself to come into judgment. The word judgment is *Shapah,* which has the idea of making a determination. The word *whether* is *Im* which could be translated *if.* The verse could read that God will judge or determine every act, even what we create from our imagination, to determine if it is in harmony with Him or not.

The writer also says that everything hidden will be judged as well. Hidden is the word *Alam,* which is also the word for *everlasting.* Do we ever stop to think that our creative acts could last forever? God created the world in His imagination. He created us in His image and gave us an imagination as well. It is with our imagination that we picture a bridge and then build it; just as God pictured a tree and then created it. We are reminded in this passage that we will be judged in how we use this gift to create. If you are a songwriter, you can write a song that will be hurtful to God and others, or will honor Him. You can paint a picture that will either bring glory or dishonor to God. It is your choice.

God gave us the imagination to create ways to honor Him and bring us into intimacy with Him. Because of our creative gifts from God, we can relate to Him as no other creature can, or we can bring hurt and dishonor to Him as no other creature can. It is our choice, and God will make the final judgment in how we use our gifts.

To sign up for Chaim Bentorah's free daily Hebrew Word study, explore his books, and learn more about his in-depth biblical Hebrew online learning platform, please visit: https://www.chaimbentorah.com/

Chapter 17

PEACE THROUGH JUDGMENT

Every decision is a judgment: a righteous judgment or an evil judgment!

Judgment and peace are rarely seen as symbiotic. The very word *judgment* can send fear up the spine of the person raised in religious legalism. In fact, far too many believers see God as an angry, old man racing toward the world with two stone tablets from which he will judge and punish mankind! *Judgment* is another word that, because of an incorrect definition, has been used to grossly misrepresent God.

The blame for our repulsion of judgment can't be laid solely on the back of the church. The perversion of judgment is a necessary pursuit for those dragging us into a one-world government that will ultimately facilitate the coming of the antichrist and his worldwide persecution.

In order for the world to become vulnerable to the power-hungry elite, justice must be perverted. For justice to be perverted, it must become an inhumane process. Justice and judgment necessitate absolute truth and morals. It's inherent in fallen nature that good and evil be subjective, not absolute. Once judgment is perverted, good will be called evil, and evil will be called good, foundations will be destroyed, and the righteous will have no place of safety in the earth.

As the world plunges deeper into socialism, mankind loses all logic and value for a just and free society. Humanism, communism, socialism and progressivism are outgrowths of Luciferian philosophy. The underlying intention is chaos, destabilization, mass wickedness and absolute control by the elite, alienating man from the lordship of Jesus.

The argument for permissive, liberal laws is based on the socialistic concept that we're not personally responsible for our life and subsequent actions—society is responsible. After all, we didn't choose our family, the cities we were born or our economic status. Since they deny the basics of creation, they don't believe we can change our life trajectory by simply making responsible decisions. And… they absolutely do not believe we can be born-again.

In light of "man-made science," we have no right to hold anyone accountable for their destructive actions. Amazingly, that position only holds if you're not a Christian or a person with moral standards. Why the duplicity? Because people like us are the problem. By preaching the "gospel," we torment those with no control over their behavior and make them worse.

The fact that we label an act of infidelity as adultery, means that we're "in judgment," making us self-righteous hypocrites. When we "call out" someone who is twisting the facts, especially of those with different viewpoints, then we're "in judgment"; therefore, we're the troublemakers and tormentors spreading division and hatred! In other words, if we, in any way, require a person to be personally responsible, we're a danger to society that should be silenced by any means!

> We compare one child to another, which is, in their minds, a form of judgment.

Stop and think, we've become so judgmentally perverted that, in some schools, children can't be acknowledged for winning a competition. We compare one child to another, which is, in their minds, a form of judgment. Judgment requires absolute standards, like the person who crosses the finish line first wins! All extreme perversions of judgment, like all antichrist philosophies, have hidden agendas that are so corrupt and far-reaching, the average person wouldn't believe any sane person could work such a seditious, despicable agenda.

The frightening, vile word *judgment,* hated so much by the world, merely means *to decide*! A judge in a courtroom uses the law to decide if people are innocent or guilty of breaking the law. Since justice is no longer served in our courtrooms, the question isn't, "Did this person break the law?"

The question now is, "Does this person have a good excuse for breaking the law, i.e., is there someone else to blame?" In a horrific deception, under the banner of mercy, absolutes are destroyed, subjective relativity becomes the norm, and good and evil are as we see it!

The root of all wickedness began in the Garden when Adam and Eve declared, "We don't trust God to decide for us anymore; we want to decide for ourselves!" We arrogantly consider ourselves to be more righteous, just, and fair than God! Every evil that's ever happened in all of human history is the result of people someone deciding what they would or would not do. They could have decided something else but instead chose to feed their lust-fueled perversion for greed or power, despite the pain and suffering they brought to others. Every law that hurts our nation, our economy, or any other aspect negatively affecting our quality of life was made by a politician profiting from the cost to its citizens—us!

The three things we must acknowledge if we're ever to have a just world are:

1. Every person has freedom of choice.
2. Every person should have to live in the consequences of their choices.
3. When people change their hearts, their choices will change.

The eternal judgments will occur at the time when every person must give an account of their life. It's when we encounter the eternal consequences of our decisions, not when God decides our eternal fate. The three final judgments are:

1. **The Judgment seat of Christ** is where all believers will have their works judged. It's not a judgment about salvation; it's a judgment about what we did with the treasure God gave us in Jesus. Did we help others? Did we serve and minister to those who needed help, love, mercy, and correction?

    1 Cor. 3:9 -15 provides a glimpse into the ultimate act of mercy which, by the way, if there wasn't absolute good and evil, there could be no such thing as mercy! The quality of our service to mankind is characterized as gold, silver, and precious stones versus wood, hay, and straw, quite frightening for the person with a twisted concept of God's judgment. But listen to this:

Each one's work will become clear; for the Day will declare it, because it will be revealed by fire; and the fire will test each one's work, of what sort it is. If anyone's work which he has built on it endures, he will receive a reward. If anyone's work is burned, he will suffer loss; but he himself will be saved, yet so as through fire. (1 Cor. 3:13-15)

We don't pass through the fire; our works pass through the fire. Wood, hay and straw are that which is unacceptable to God and are subsequently burned; thus, all we take with us when we stand before the King are those things that are acceptable. We will then receive our just rewards… but only for those things that are acceptable and praiseworthy. (Evidently, heaven won't be a socialist society.)

2. **The Great White Throne Judgment** is where those who decided to reject the righteousness of God will give an account of their works. Notice that in both of these judgments, those present are there because of their judgments (decisions), not God's.

   So why aren't believers present for the White Throne Judgment when they have sins and failures for which they must give account. Simple!

3. **We've already experienced the judgment** of our old man and joyfully accepted the sentence of death on all he was so we could live the resurrected life now. We made a judgment (decision). With respect to God's commandments teaching us to walk in love, we decide to trust in the mercy and salvation He offers through Jesus instead of trusting in our own works.

   Without God, we already abide in death. Refusal to accept His life through Jesus is our decision (judgment) to abide in death and reject life. When we accept God's judgment, because *"All have sinned and fall short of the glory of God."* (Rom. 3:23) and *"By the deeds of the law no flesh will be justified in His sight."* (Rom. 3:20), we *"Pass from death into life."* (John 5:24) We chose to stand before God, plead guilty, and receive His forgiveness offered freely in Jesus.

The Apostle Paul told us to take communion with the same mind-set the Israelites used when observing the feasts (1 Cor. 11:24-32). They observed the feasts by looking back to when God delivered them from Egypt. Believers are instructed to take communion in remembrance of what Jesus did on the cross. The Israelites were also to look forward to the time the feasts would be fulfilled in the Messiah. We take communion looking forward to the second coming of the Messiah.

Paul specifically emphasizes the importance of taking communion in a *"worthy manner."* Sadly, religion took what should have been an activation of our faith and turned it into something negative and condemning. We've been taught that participating in communion without resolving every sin would cause God to smite us because to do so would be to receive in an *"unworthy manner."*

As it turns out, the unworthy, or irreverent, manner of taking communion is to do so without doing these two things: 1) examining ourselves and 2) failure to discern the blood and body of Christ. This word **examine** isn't self-scrutiny to find what's wrong with us; it's an exhortation *to find ourselves approved.*[8] How and why would we seek to find ourselves approved? Simple! By discerning the effects of the blood and body of Christ, we can only find ourselves approved!

> With our mind renewed and our conscience purged, we look ahead to the second coming with no fear of standing before our Savior.

If we discern the blood of Jesus applied to our life, we're reminded that we've been washed in His blood. Our conscience is cleansed. Fear, guilt, and condemnation evaporate. When we discern that He carried our sin and bore our sicknesses in His body, we can find healing. When we follow the direction of the religious, however, we look inward for fault and partake in an unworthy manner. The devastation in our heart, mind, and body is the cause of the sickness and death to which Paul refers.

In addition to the peace and joy we experience concerning our standing before God in this very moment, we're also reminding ourselves that we were crucified with Christ, delivering us from the power of sin and raising us up in newness of life. With our mind renewed and our conscience purged, we look ahead to the second coming with no fear of standing before our Savior. We're delivered from condemnation!

Condemnation is *the fear and expectation of judgment.* When we don't maintain a clear conscience by consistently revisiting the cross, we often find ourselves with an abiding sense of dread. We continually expect

---

8   Examine: to recognize as genuine after examination, to approve, deem worthy. Biblesoft, *Thayer's Greek Lexicon*, (Online: Biblesoft, 2006).

things to go wrong and experience anything from a subtle sense of doom and gloom to a paranoid hysteria, because our hearts aren't established in the love, grace, and peace of God.

Hebrews 6:1-2 lists the foundational doctrines of the New Covenant that must be the basis for our every doctrinal belief, and among them is the doctrine of eternal judgment. Under the influence of religion, we will see the phrase *eternal judgment* and cringe in fear, but under the influence of the grace, peace, and love of God, we will see the same phrase and rejoice in peace!

Ask yourself this question, "Do I have so little trust for the character and nature of God that I assume any part of His being to be unjust?" Maybe it's time to admit, "God, I really don't know how to trust Your justice, but I want to trust You. Lead me to the place where I learn to ask questions and look for answers without questioning Your justice."

Jesus came, not just to save you from hell, but to give you and incredible quality of life here. There is a realm that is offered to us all. Jesus called it The Kingdom of Heaven; basically that means Heaven on Earth. If you have the courage to leave the average Christian life behind and become a disciple who follows Jesus whole-heartedly and experiences the best life possible check out my book and audio series *Heaven on Earth* (https://www.impactministries.com/heavenonearth/).

GRACE

When we say Yes, God gives us the power to do what He asks!

Chapter 18

PITCHING A TENT IN GOD'S CAMP

(Chaim Bentorah)

Ephesians 2:8: *"For by grace are ye saved through faith; and that not of yourselves: [it is] the gift of God."*

Genesis 6: 8: *"But Noah found grace in the eyes of the LORD."*

I believe we all know that grace means *unmerited favor*. In Greek, the word for *grace* is *Charis,* which means favor, freely given or extended, always leaning toward. In Aramaic, the word is *Taybutha,* which has the idea of favor and goodness. In Talmudic literature, it is used as a sign of recognition. Let's hold that thought "a sign of recognition" and go to the Hebrew.

In Genesis 6:8, the Hebrew word for grace is given in its Semitic root, which is just two letters. It is the word *Chen (Cheth Nun).* I believe the Semitic root is used to make a play on the word Noah, which is *Chen* spelled backward (*Nun Cheth*) – *Noach,* which means rest.

The root word for grace is often given as *Cheth Nun. Nun* means favor. But Jewish rabbis will challenge this and say the Hebrew triliteral root is *Cheth Nun Hei.* This means to encamp and set up tents. I believe the use of the Semitic root indicates that both Hebrew roots were intended to be used.

It is not enough to say that Noah found favor in the eyes of God. What does that really mean? How did he find favor in the eyes of God? If we do a little wordplay, *Noah* tells us, he found grace or favor in God by resting in God, doing nothing. Paul tells us that we are saved by grace, not by our works. We are saved by just resting in God, doing nothing but applying faith. Even the word itself shows this. The *Cheth* is bonding or forming an intimate relationship with God, and the *Nun* tells us that this is done by faith. We cannot earn it, or work for it; it is a gift, *Donon* in the Greek.

Still, that doesn't show us how Noah found this grace. But when we go to the very Semitic origin of *Chen* as an encampment and/or pitching tents, we get an idea. In ancient times, as it is today, encampments were a family thing. The Bedouin groups were tribes or families, and they would travel as a family. There is safety in numbers, and so they would travel, and set up camp in a large family group. They would pitch their tents in a large circle, setting up a wall surrounding the families. No one was allowed to enter their encampment because they did not trust anyone outside their family. The only way to find refuge in an encampment would be to show you were a member of the family.

This tradition even follows throughout the world. There have been many cowboy movies made where a white man was allowed to live with a tribe of Indians, but only if he became a "blood brother" so the old Western movies taught me. Nonetheless, this was a practice that one could find refuge in a Bedouin camp only if he became a member of the family.

Grace is unmerited favor; God extending to everyone the privilege to become a member of His family by being born again through the shed blood of His Son Jesus. Just as a person has to prove worthy of becoming a member of a tribe to find rest in that tribe or family, we become worthy of becoming a member of God's family by becoming born again. We find rest in the safety of the encampment by only believing that God's Son shed His blood for us. It is by faith, and it is a gift, a *Donon*, that we receive, for no other reason than God loves us.

There is one other definition of *Chen* and even *Charis* other than grace; it is acceptance.

We approach the camp of God and request to enter the safety of that encampment. God simply says: "You have to be my child to enter. You must prove worthy." Then God's Son Jesus steps forward and says: "This one is worthy because I died for this person." Then Jesus turns to us and says: "Do you want to be a child of God and enter our encampment?" Now it is up to you, either say yes or no.

To sign up for Chaim Bentorah's free daily Hebrew Word study, explore his books, and learn more about his in-depth biblical Hebrew online learning platform, please visit: https://www.chaimbentorah.com/

Chapter 19

GRACE AND PEACE

Believers are reminded to remain in grace and peace more than any other truth!

Throughout Scripture, we see God's grace being expressed to His followers. The concept of grace in the Hebrew is similar to the meaning of the word *grace* in the New Testament Greek. As always, the Hebrew definitions provide the foundational truth of words and terms later used in the Greek.

God gives and expresses Himself out of who He is. His actions can't be separated from His character, which is one of the many reasons why the Old Testament believer should have begun all studies of Scripture with the names of God. The Old Testament word for **grace** translates as *favor, grace, elegance, and acceptance*.[9] The root word incorporates the idea of *bending or stooping in kindness to an inferior*.[10] Contrary to the religious concept of an angry, hard-to-please God, or its preferred definition *to garner favor*, the language and actions imply that He stoops down to us mere mortals to extend kindness, favor, and acceptance.

Most of what we've learned about the Old Covenant offerings could be

---
9   Brown, Driver, and Briggs, Online Bible Thayer's Greek Lexicon and Hebrew Lexicon, (Ontario: Woodside Bible Fellowship, 1993).
10   Biblesoft, *New Exhaustive Strong's Concordance* (Online: Biblesoft, 2006).

one reason we misunderstand the God of grace, who longs to give us favor. It seems the Hebrews resisted God as He revealed Himself and related to Him the same way the rest of the world related to their pagan gods.

Offerings to a pagan god were not only to appease their continual wrath but to convince them to draw near and bestow favor upon the worshipper. The greater the sacrifice, the more likely the god would respond. This mind-set led to human sacrifices. After all, what more could be given? God warned them not to relate to Him the same way the pagans related to their gods.

The sacrifices for the Hebrews weren't designed to get God to draw near to them. His promise was sure never to leave or forsake them (Deut. 31:6). They were drawing near to Him in their own heart. They should have realized it wasn't God who had abandoned the relationship; they were! Their offerings weren't intended to convince God to come back to them; they were meant to influence their hearts to recover value for their relationship with God.

Like everything else in the New Covenant, grace is better, just as there are better promises and better sacrifices, an easier and lighter way with Christ in us, and more. In the New Covenant, we're baptized into the body of Christ; and, yes, this is a spiritual reality, not a mere metaphoric concept. In Christ, we share in everything He has, everything He's done, and everything He will do! But it doesn't stop there; not only are we in Him, but He is in us by the Holy Spirit! This means that He expresses all He is through us!

Grace in the New Covenant expands into the fact that His power is in us; we can do everything He can do! Remember, the same power that raised Jesus from the dead works to empower us with resurrection life (Rom. 8:11). As such, *grace* isn't merely favor, but it's also His power, His capacity, and His ability… because He's in us!

The Apostle Peter refers to the *"Manifold grace of God."* (1 Pet. 4:10) Grace isn't a one-dimensional reality. The word **manifold** means *various or multifaceted*. Limiting grace to *unmerited favor* isn't incorrect, but it's an extreme minimization of its totality. We have favor with God, and, as such, all He does is unmerited. We receive nothing from Him as a payment for our works. In the New Covenant, grace comes to us by unmerited favor, but that's not precisely what it is. Grace is the power, capacity, ability, and strength of God that we access by faith! (This is explained more in the next chapter.)

Salvation is a work of grace, i.e., God's capacity to be righteous and His power to make us righteous. The born-again experience is a work of grace—His ability! The gifts of the Holy Spirit are a work of grace. Paul indicated that he fulfilled his ministry by the grace of God working in Him (Eph. 3:7). Anything God calls us to do, or anything we desire to do in our service to Him and others, is empowered in us as a work of faith and grace. Even the capacity to grow in our faith for grace is a work of grace, which takes us from grace to grace (John 1:16).

One of the most important aspects of grace in the New Covenant is the power to live righteously.

> *Where sin abounded, grace abounded much more, so that as sin reigned in death, even so grace might reign through righteousness to eternal life through Jesus Christ our Lord.* (Rom. 5:20-21)

It doesn't matter how great our sin is or how powerful the grip it has on our life; when we choose to live in righteousness, grace gives us the power to do so!

God wants the promise to be sure to all. In His loving-kindness, He knew that many would fail in our struggle with the flesh. In the New Covenant, He was able to make the promises sure to all who would believe, "*Therefore it is of faith that it might be according to grace, so that the promise might be sure to all*." (Rom. 4:16) If we believe we're the righteousness of God in Christ, we become empowered to live as the righteousness of God.

> In Jesus, you can pick any godly trait you desire with the assurance that Christ in you activates that trait to manifest.

In Jesus, you can pick any godly trait you desire with the assurance that Christ in you activates that trait to manifest. No matter how strong the opposing temptation or sin may be, you'll experience a superior act of grace than you've ever experienced to counteract the power of temptation to sin. In fact, any weakness you desire to overcome by the grace of God will become your greatest strength!

Nearly every Epistle in the New Testament opens with the words "*Grace and peace to you from God* ."[11] Theologians suggest this to be a friendly introduction with no theological value. I strongly disagree! It's my opinion that grace and peace were so crucial to understanding and applying what was written in these letters that we have to be continually reminded that God is at peace with us through the Lord Jesus, and His grace is at work in us!

Grace is the greatest power available to man. Yet, we have limited it to unmerited favor. Grace is much more than unmerited favor. Grace is the power that worked in Jesus making Him able to be and do all He did in His earthly life and ministry. To learn more about God's incredible grace and peace, visit: https://www.impactministries.com/product/grace-the-power-to-change/, for my ground-breaking, audio series and bestselling book called *Grace: The Power To Change*.

---

11   James B. Richards, *Grace The Power to Change*, (New Kensington: Whitaker House, 1993).

FAITH

Effortless power flows through the one who believes!

Chapter 20

WORKS ARE BUILT INTO FAITH

(Chaim Bentorah)

Genesis 15:6: *"And he (Abraham) believed the Lord and He counted it as righteousness."*

John 3:16: *"For God so loved the world, that he gave his only begotten Son, that whosoever believeth in him should not perish, but have everlasting life."*

James 2:20: *"But wilt thou know, O vain man, that faith without works is dead?"*

John 3:16 is the hallmark verse for salvation, Just believe in God, and we will not perish but have everlasting life. That has always troubled me, as it sounded contradictory to James 2:19, 20. *"The devils believe and tremble,"* and *"faith without works is dead."*

So what gives? Jesus said all we need to do is believe (Gr. *Pisteuo*), but James says we must have faith (Gr. *Pisteuo*) *and* works. I think the answer lies in the fact that Jesus spoke Aramaic, and James wrote his book in Greek. When Jesus said that whoever believes, he did not say *Pisteuo,* for he was not speaking in Greek but in Aramaic. According to my Aramaic Bible, He said *'Emen,* which is identical to the Hebrew word rendered for faith or belief, *'Aman.*

The Talmud teaches that trusting in God is more important than anything else. One may keep all the laws of Torah, follow every ritual, but it is only belief *'Emen*, which will ultimately save the individual.

Remember how Saul lost his kingdom because he performed a sacrifice before a battle rather than wait for Samuel? Samuel was late, Saul's army was deserting him, but Saul would not go to war until the sacrifice was offered, so he did it himself. What was his sin? Disobedience, of course, but I never heard a Christian teacher give the core reason. I had to go to Jewish literature to find it. It was that Saul did not believe or *'Emen* in God. This is more than just believing that God exists. The Bible says that devils *believe* and tremble. That hardly sounds like this *belief* or *'Emen* is counted as righteousness. The word used in the Greek for *believe* in James 2:19 is *Pisteuo*, which means to have *faith in, trust in or have belief*. So why is it that the devils' *Pisteuo* is not counted as righteousness?

The reason is that *Pisteuo* is not the same as the Hebrew word *'Aman*, which is used in Genesis 15:6. I don't think there is an appropriate word in Greek or in English to render the word *'Aman*.

> Jesus would not have to mention works because works was already built into the faith.

You can only describe *'Aman*. That is why James says that faith without works is dead, he is saying *Pisteuo* without works is dead. If this were written in Hebrew, he would have used *'Aman*. Then, like Jesus, in John 3:16, he would not have to mention works because works was already built into the word *'Aman*. *'Aman* is *Pisteuo* and *Ergon (works)* all wrapped in one word.

It is essential to understand that the Greek word for works is *Ergon,* and it does not just mean good deeds, but it is a *work which fulfills an inner desire*. What is this *work* that fills an inner desire? Ah, the Hebrew word *'Aman*, and its twin Aramaic word, that Jesus used in John 3:16. *'Emen* gives us the answer to that question.

The Talmud teaches that if a drowning man suddenly spots a tree within his reach, which part of the tree does he lunge for? Not the branches, for they will break under his weight, instead he grabs the roots of the tree. Belief in God is similar to the strong roots of a tree; it is the basis and foundation of the entire tree. That is our salvation in Jesus Christ, which is what it means to believe *'Emen* or *'Aman* in Jesus.

The Jewish sages understood the Semitic root of the word *'Aman*. It is found in the clay tablets of the Akkadian cuneiform, the Sumerians, and the Ugaritic, the Persian, Phoenician, and Canaanite languages. It is the word *AMN*, used to describe a mother nursing a baby. Why would the Hebrews use the word for a mother nursing a baby to describe their trust or belief in God? Why would Jesus use such a word as that which will give us everlasting life?

Consider the dynamics involved in nursing a baby. The mother must cradle the baby in her arms. The baby is in the total protection of its mother. The mother is providing sustenance to the baby directly from herself, not from a spoon or cup, and it is her own milk, not the milk of a goat or cow. Artists, in depicting a mother nursing will have the mother looking at her baby with total love in her eyes and the baby looking up to its mother with absolute trust and dependence in its eyes. Through the nursing process, a deep bonding takes place between the mother and child.

When we trust or believe in God, we are not just acknowledging His existence. To believe in God as Jesus said in John 3:16 means we must become like a baby in a mother's arms. It is as natural as a baby reaching out to its mother, as natural as receiving nourishment and strength as a baby receives from its mother.

To receive everlasting life, we are to simply to be cradled in the arms of Jesus, looking up at him and seeing nothing but Him as He looks lovingly down on us, providing nourishment and strength from His own being. To that baby who is *'Aman* with its mother, nothing else in the world exists but its mother. And to the mother, nothing else in the world is more important than that baby in her arms. Nothing else in the world is more important to Jesus than we are when we are cradled in His arms.

The baby does not have to behave to get its mother's love and be fed by its mother. The baby must do nothing but rest in its mother's arms and let its mother love on him. Nothing else is required. That baby has naturally performed its *Ergon (works)*. The work in salvation is not good deeds, going to church, throwing money in an offering plate. *Ergon* is doing a work which fulfills your inner desire. Our *Ergon* with God is *'Aman,* that is fulfilling our inner desire to be held and nourished by God.

If a baby ignores its mother's attempts to hold it and nourish it, it will perish. If we ignore Jesus' attempts to hold us in His arms and nourish us, we too will perish and not have everlasting life. According to Jesus, the only way we can have eternal life is to submit ourselves to God and let Him cradle us in His arms and nourish us, for just as life flows through that mother into the baby, so too does eternal life flow through Jesus into us. We just have to be willing to receive it. That is salvation.

To sign up for Chaim Bentorah's free daily Hebrew Word study, explore his books, and learn more about his in-depth biblical Hebrew online learning platform, please visit: https://www.chaimbentorah.com/

Chapter 21

TRUSTING GOD

We can only trust those we know well enough to believe they are trustworthy!

Religionists of various persuasions would have us believe everything about faith except its most important trait. For some, faith is primarily how to get what we want from God; more specifically, our attempt to persuade God to respond to our needs and requests. If that's the case, then faith is a form of **dead works** (*works to solicit a response from God*). Since the first two foundations of the New Covenant are *repentance from dead works* and *faith toward God*, this religious concept of faith can't be accurate!

Until we repent (change our mind about dead works), we can't understand what faith toward God is. One of its principles reveals that faith doesn't come from understanding; understanding comes from faith. Until we trust what God has revealed about Himself, we'll never understand the rest of the process. Dead works are the things we do, sacrifice, or perform to invoke God to respond. If He were to respond to our bids, then nothing He gives us is a gift but rather a payment for services rendered.

Repentance from dead works can sometimes be confusing because dead works and good works can be the same action(s). What separates one from the other is motive. God abhorred the Old Testament sacrifices from people who just wanted to get something from Him. To bring a sacrifice or do a good deed to get God to respond means we believe Him to be no different than pagan gods. Conversely, good works, which could be the same action as dead works, are those things we do motivated by love for God or in response to His love for us. Here's the paradox: we're to repent of dead works, but we're His workmanship created unto good works (Eph. 2:10).

Faith isn't what moves God to respond to us; ***faith*** is our *response of trust to Him*. Faith in God believes in and acts on His instructions as prescriptions for an abundant life. When we trust Him, we believe He's given us all things for our benefit.

Relationships are built on honest communication and trust. God gives us everything we'll ever need to know Him and asks only one thing, "Trust me; trust what I say about myself!" Hebrews 11:6, *"But without faith it is impossible to please Him, for he who comes to God must believe that He is, and that He is a rewarder of those who diligently seek Him."*

The primary concept of faith is trust and trustworthiness![12] Faith seems to be a continuum of how we see and respond to God. James 2:26 says, *"Faith without works is dead."* One-dimensional theologians find themselves arguing about faith versus works because they fail to grasp the dynamics of heart beliefs. Beliefs of the heart produce a shift in our sense of self,[13] out of which our behavior flows effortlessly as an extension of who we believe we are; therefore, when we fail to produce actions based on our stated beliefs, we're operating ***dead faith***. It's in our mouths, and it may even be in the Bible, but it's not in our heart.

Faith trusts God and in His trustworthiness to His Word, the evidence of which is always obedience. Faith isn't a generality about God nor our subjective opinion of who God is. It's trust in the fact that God is who He declares Himself to be: good, loving, merciful, and forgiving... always!

The following are just six of the many irrefutable expressions of absolute certainty concerning the fact that God is good, and He rewards those who earnestly seek Him (Heb. 11:6):

1. **His Creation.** God created a habitable world, and everything in the universe is coordinated specifically to sustain life on Planet Earth.

---

12 Pistós: a. "trusting" (also with the nuance of "obedient") and b. "trustworthy," i.e., faithful, reliable. Gerhard Kittel, *Theological Dictionary of the New Testament,* (Grand Rapids: Eerdmans Publishing, 1985).
13 Jim Richards, *Moving You Invisible Boundaries,* (Travelers Rest: True Potential, 2013).

Man was His very last creation; God having prepared all things for his arrival. Man's first day alive was a day of rest and enjoying the Creator and His provision. No one prayed or used faith to convince God to be so generously proactive.

2. **His Plan**. When man chose to rebel against his Creator, declaring himself to be his own god, the One True God implemented His strategy for their escape from spiritual destruction. Out of His foreknowledge, mercy, and lovingkindness, God initiated His plan for a Savior—a plan originated before the foundation of the World (Eph. 1:4).

3. **His Names**. God revealed every essential aspect of His character, nature, and intentions toward man through His names. He made sure we had a solid foundation for understanding and interpreting His every Word and action.

4. **His Commandments**. Despite the religious distortions concerning God's commandments, they were the most humane instructions for civil order ever given. History proves that when nations reject the moral standards of God's commandments, they decline into moral, ethical, and political corruption and decay that erodes the quality living in every area of life.

5. **His Model**. God sent Jesus so we would 1) have a living expression of the Father and 2) see what we could be or do if we followed His teachings and example. Jesus' life removed the veil of mysticism that hid the true character and nature of God so He could be known, understood, and experienced as He really is.

6. **His Propitiation**. The propitiation was the ultimate expression of God's character, nature, and love. By becoming our sin, taking all of its consequences, dying the death we deserve, conquering sin, death, hell, and the devil, and obtaining an inheritance He shares freely with us, God's character, nature, and love is undeniable.

Based on these fulfilled expressions of love, mercy, and kindness, we can trust God's promise that, even when the majority of the world's population turns to the antichrist and his efforts to savagely destroy all who believe in the God of the Bible, Jesus will return—not to destroy the world as religionists have taught, but to establish His kingdom here on earth. The remainder of humanity will experience God's love, justice, and mercy before entering into eternity. For one thousand years, we'll see how the world could have been had we only trusted God and His wisdom.

The New Covenant has one doctrinal promise, however, that delineates the religionists from believers. Religionists believe in their personal version of Jesus, while believers accept the biblical account of Christ, as clearly identified first in Isaiah 53. It's such an outlandish promise that God Himself called it *"The stumbling stone of the gospel."* (Isa. 8:14-15)

The New Covenant promise was so far beyond their carnal-minded capacity or willingness to believe, God called upon prophets to prepare us hundreds of years before Jesus came,

> *What shall we say then? That Gentiles, who did not pursue righteousness, have attained to righteousness, even the righteousness of faith; but Israel, pursuing the law of righteousness, has not attained to the law of righteousness. Why? Because they did not seek it by faith, but as it were, by the works of the law. For they stumbled at that stumbling stone. As it is written: "Behold, I lay in Zion a stumbling stone and rock of offense, And whoever believes on Him will not be put to shame.* (Rom 9:30-33)

Every believer who's given much study to the New Testament knows Abraham is the father of faith. As in all things, religionists incorrectly limit Abraham's faith to getting what he wanted: a son! No doubt, having a son was one incredible goal of his faith, but that wasn't the totality of his faith, *"And he believed in the Lord, and He accounted it to him for righteousness."* (Gen. 15:6) God promised Abraham that he would produce an heir that would become a multitude, and, through his heir, all the nations of the earth would be blessed. The nation that would come from him would inhabit the land of Canaan.

To move forward, I must educate you by briefly deviating on this point. God's promise to Abraham is why Muslims will fight to the total destruction of their own people in order to completely annihilate the Jews—the same reason every atheist politician wants Israel to surrender to Islamic terrorism. Israel's occupation of Canaan is a testament to the Muslims that they worship a false God. To the liberals and atheists, it means the God of the Bible is real; therefore, His moral values are absolute. All who seek to destroy Israel work a secret, evil agenda! Now, we can move forward.

On the continuum between liberalism and conservatism is a constant battle. What is righteousness? What does it look like in application? Is

God's definition of righteousness a plausible definition for the 21st century? How righteous must we be to inherit a particular promise? These questions war in the minds of Christians, particularly when faced with tragedy—the crowning point of hesitation, when they begin to ask themselves the wrong questions resulting in condemnation and self-fulfilling prophesies of their own making, "Have I prayed enough? Am I spiritual enough? Am I good enough for God to hear my request?"

The previous passage in Romans 9 should end these questions and lead us immediately to a response of faith, "Because I am in Jesus, I am righteous. I didn't get this righteousness by works or performance; I received it because I trusted what God said, what Jesus did, and who I am in Him!"

The book of Romans is one of the most important epistles for learning how to be a Christian without becoming religious. Understanding Romans requires an understanding of the Old Testament, which foretold of the New Covenant and explained its provisions. Sadly, much of the teaching about Romans disturbingly misses the mark; nevertheless, we'll look to another incredibly clear passage in Romans 5:1-2,

> *"Therefore, having been justified* (made righteous) *by faith* (trusting what God said about Jesus), *we have peace* (a tranquil state of mind that comes from knowing God's protection and resources are available to me) *with* (with, in, and through) *God through our Lord Jesus Christ* (in Jesus, I share in His inheritance), *through whom also we have access by faith* (believing I'm righteous opens my access) *into this grace in which we stand* (free, unmerited access into the strength, power, capacity, and ability of God called *grace*, which makes me able to live righteously), *and rejoice* (joyfully boast in thankfulness and worship) *in hope* (confident expectation) *of the glory of God* (the view, the opinion, the reality of God, because I choose it as my reality)."

> He sees you whole, complete, happy, satisfied and living in righteousness, peace, and joy.

I recommend prayerfully reading this verse several times and considering the more appropriate translations and applications I've added based on the most reliable research sources.

God's **glory** is many things, all of which have their root in His goodness. God has a view and opinion of you, one in which you share in all that Jesus obtained for you through His death, burial, and resurrection. He sees you whole, complete, happy, satisfied and living in righteousness, peace, and joy. This isn't an unfounded imagination; it's a reality you can step into the moment you start believing in all that God says you are, have, and can do because you're in Jesus. You'll choose a reality based on the opinion you trust the most: yours, your denomination's, your religious or non-religious culture's, or the Word of God, which has only ever been proven true despite the millions of attempts to prove it wrong.

God's calling you to a relationship which starts by being willing to trust Him. Like all friendships, the longer you walk together, the more you'll experience the consistency of His character and the more you'll trust Him!

In 1983, on the verge of death from a congenital kidney disease, mountain of debt for over three years of surgeries and experimental drugs, I developed one of the most powerful tools I ever created. The Prayer Organizer is a tool that connects the Names of God, to the life and ministry of Jesus, all the promises associated with each name, our identity in Jesus, and how to establish all that in our hearty. It is designed to help you have faith in God's true identity, see and connect to God as He really is, and bring His promises to life this may be just what you've been search and praying for. Ten of thousands of people around the world have transformed their prayer life and their heart using this incredible tool. Please visit: https://www.impactministries.com/product/the-prayer-organizer/, for more information on a proven and powerful resource for personal transformation called: *The Prayer Organizer*.

SHALOM

Peace is the unspoken language of God, until we have peace nothing else works as it should!

Chapter 22

PEACE PERFECTED

(Chaim Bentorah)

Isaiah 26:3: *"Thou wilt keep him in perfect peace, whose mind is stayed on thee: because he trusteth in thee."*

One morning on my disability bus, a woman, Barbara was her name, told me that she had two heart attacks within the last year. One was in the hospital, and she died, until the staff revived her. I asked her rather flippantly, "Did you see the white light?"

She got quiet and then said: "You know, I read your book. I have told very few people this, and they usually pass me off as crazy, but I think you will believe me." She said: "I saw paradise."

I glanced over, and her eyes were sparkling; there was a glow about her. As I encouraged her to tell me more, everyone else on the bus became quiet, She said; "I can't describe it. I saw flowers, but nothing like here on earth, they were so beautiful, flowers like I have never seen." Then she said: "Oh, the peace! Never have I felt such peace. I was free; I felt no pain, no physical hindrances, and I could walk effortlessly. I saw my mother, she has been dead for years, but there she was, and I was talking with her. Then I saw what looked like a picnic table. A man with dark hair was sitting at the table. All I knew was that I just wanted to be with Him. I felt loved like I had never felt loved and peace like I had never felt peace. Suddenly I was whisked back to the hospital."

Peace Perfected

I don't remember it, but the staff said that when I woke up, I was angry, screaming that I wanted to go back, and they had to restrain me." She said she eventually realized that they did not bring her back, but God sent her back for reasons she does not know. I don't think there was a dry eye on that bus as she told her story.

She kept talking about this perfect peace and her longing to return. This time to fall into the arms of Jesus, and experience that perfect complete love. She said she never dreamed that God was so perfect in loving. When she finished her story, I queued up the song "Home Where I Belong" on my iPod. I glanced over and saw her weeping as she listened to those words, "They say heaven is pretty and living here is too but if I had the choice between the two, I'd go home, going home where I belong."

If she reminded me of anything, it is that I don't belong in this world. When everyone got off my bus, I pulled over for a few minutes and wept. I wept over all the loneliness I felt and the longing to be with Jesus, to be home where I belong. One day Jesus will say those wonderful words to me: "It's finished, you can come home, you can come home to stay." In that moment of weeping and homesickness, I believe I felt perfect *peace*. I understand what Barbara felt, for I believe I felt something close to the same, a perfect peace beyond anything I could ever hope to imagine.

The context of Isaiah 26:3 makes it clear that it is Jehovah who keeps us in perfect peace. Jehovah is the feminine form of God's name; it embodies His love, tenderness, caring, and peace. The word for *keep* is *Tisor*, which, in its Semitic root, has the idea of *guarding or watching over*. So, it is not so much that he is *giving us* or *keeping* us in *perfect peace*, but he is watching over us with *perfect peace*.

He will keep us in *perfect peace*. The word *perfect* is not found in the Hebrew here. It is simply the word *shalom*, repeated two times. Hebrew grammar does not have comparative and superlative adjectives like *good, better, best*. To show degrees, it just repeats a word. So, this is not only peace, but the best peace, better than the world can give according to Jesus (John 14:27). God, Himself is at *perfect peace* or the *best peace*.

Jesus is this *perfect peace*. The way we gain access to this *perfect peace* is by having our *minds stayed on him*. The word, mind, in Hebrew, used here is *Yeser*. This is a play on the word for *keep*. Both are spelled with a *Sade* and *Resh*, which represent a *humble submission* to the Holy Spirit. The word,

Yeser comes from a Semitic root *Sbr*, which is a word used for *imagination*. God guards over our *imaginations* with *perfect peace*.

It is sort of like when you notice you have a physical problem. Your first thought (*imagination*) is that you have cancer or some fatal illness. You worry and fret, and you have no peace. You go to a doctor who smiles and says: "You're okay." Suddenly, all your fears and worries disappear, you sigh with relief. If the doctor says you are okay, what do you have to worry about? His calm, peaceful response reassures you.

This is the way it is with God. When we face a frightening situation or crisis, we are fearful and worried. We go to God and He says: "Hey, I'm in control, it's okay." Suddenly, it is okay.

Maybe Barbara experienced a peace greater than I felt. I hope so. I hope I have just a small taste of *perfect peace, Shalom Shalom*.

To sign up for Chaim Bentorah's free daily Hebrew Word study, explore his books, and learn more about his in-depth biblical Hebrew online learning platform, please visit: https://www.chaimbentorah.com/

Chapter 23

PEACE THAT DEFIES CIRCUMSTANCES

Peace is the fruit of trusting God, regardless of the circumstances!

One of the aspects of God's temperament that's probably overlooked and lied about more than any other is this: He is the God of peace. Even those who readily acknowledge the phrase "God of Peace," seldom realize peace is such an integral aspect of His nature that His name is Jehovah-Shalom.

If we call Him the God of Peace then blame Him for trouble that befalls us, we take the name of Jehovah-Shalom in vain! He can't be the God of Peace and the author of trouble and confusion. He's one or the other.

Many times, Scripture makes a statement that should be simple to understand, but God, in His wisdom, provides a second statement that qualifies the first. Jesus said, *"Love the Lord your God with all your heart and ... soul."* (Mark 12:30) Any zealot, full of selfish ambition, could interpret that as, "If I love God more than anything else, I'm going to kill anyone who doesn't love God." Oh, but wait ... the church has already done that!

Fortunately, God qualified the first statement by the second with, *"Love your neighbor as yourself."* From this, we understand that we can't express our love for God in any way that devalues other people. Even further, this reveals that we must love (have value for) ourselves, so we can't love God in a way that demeans our dignity and worth. Why is this important? If we're created in the likeness and image of God, the way we treat His creation is a reflection of how we're really treating Him!

The God of peace gives us a list of qualifiers to help us understand what this peace should look like:

- Romans 8:6, *"To be spiritually minded is life and peace."* If we're not functioning in peace, we're operating from a carnal mind.

- James 3:18, *"Now the fruit of righteousness is sown in peace by those who make peace."* Peacemakers not only make peace, but their approach to issues also moves others into true righteousness.

- Romans 14:17, *"For the kingdom of God is not eating and drinking, but righteousness and peace and joy in the Holy Spirit."* To have heaven on earth, we must remain in peace!

- 1 Corinthians 7:15, *"But God has called us to peace."* This means that any aspect of our calling includes the call to peace. To minister, parent, or be a spouse who's not seeking to be a peacemaker is to ignore God's call to peace.

- 1 Corinthians 14:33, *"God is not the author of confusion but of peace."* When we create instability, disorder, confusion, or conflict, we aren't representing God.

- Hebrews 12:14, *"Pursue peace with all men, and holiness, without which no man shall see the Lord."* In our every interaction with others, our goal should be to promote peace.

This list of scriptures about peace could go on for pages, but the reality is: in the absence of peace, love can seldom be realized. Consider the following statements: God the Father is the God of peace. Jesus is the prince of peace. The New Covenant is the Covenant of Peace. The Gospel is called the Gospel of peace. The Kingdom to which we're called is peace.

In ancient combat, footing was absolutely essential. As long as soldiers maintained their footing in battle, there was a higher likelihood of staying alive. Likewise, every aspect of personal combat is based on balance. The accuracy of swinging a sword, thrusting a spear, throwing a punch, even wrestling an opponent to the ground depends on physical coordination, which begins and ends with the balance that comes from sound footing. An essential part of combat training would have been how to move and effectively respond to various attacks while maintaining balance, i.e., footing!

Peace That Defies Circumstances

Ephesians 6:14-18 isn't describing what we need to fight the devil. Each piece of armor represents what we need to defend ourselves against oppositional thoughts and beliefs that oppose the Truth of God. Verse 15 clearly reflects this by saying, *"And having shod your feet with the preparation of the gospel of peace."* This passage could, in effect, read this way: *"And having your feet shod with a readiness of mind that comes from a thorough preparation in the gospel of peace."*

In hand-to-hand combat, as in any personal, physical assault, the outcome is usually determined within the first few seconds. The person who strikes first nearly always wins the conflict. So, the best thing for every believer is to be vigilant… not paranoid or fearful, but vigilant to hear the voice of the Lord and follow Him in every situation without question. The one instruction Jesus gave more than any other for always overcoming was, *"Hear what the Spirit is saying."*[14]

> The person who strikes first nearly always wins the conflict.

When taken by surprise, our first reaction will nearly always determine the outcome. Please note, how quickly we respond is as important as our reaction. Hesitation usually means death! So, no matter what hits us, no matter where it comes from, no matter what it looks like, we must maintain our footing, and keeping our footing will be determined by our first response … which should be the response the Bible recommends!

If we believe the Covenant of Peace, then we realize the good news of the gospel is the fact that God is at peace with us. We're in Jesus, and we share in the covenant God made with Him. God can do nothing or allow nothing to happen to me without breaking His Covenant of Peace with Jesus. The Covenant of Peace ensures that our first response to anything negative can safely be: "This isn't from God. I am in Jesus. All the promises are mine. I am free from the curse; therefore, I send this away!"

Herein lies the confusion:

Our limited concept of the word *peace* as *a tranquil state of mind* limits our experience of the peace of God. Both the Hebrew and Greek words for *peace* are used to describe healing, prosperity, protection, and all the other promises of God that are ours in Christ. A tranquil state of mind is

---

14   Dr. Jim Richards, *Apocalypse: A Spiritual Guide to the Second Coming*, (Travelers Rest: True Potential, 2015).

founded on a thorough preparation that comes from studying, knowing, and establishing our heart in the peace of God!

When the heart is established in peace, the readiness of mind is the natural flow. Paul instructs us to:

> *Be anxious for nothing, but in everything by prayer and supplication, with thanksgiving, let your requests be made known to God; and the peace of God, which surpasses all understanding, will guard your hearts and minds through Christ Jesus.* (Phil. 4:6-7)

The word **anxious** means *concerned or troubled by the distractions that lead us away from God as our source for an abundant life*. The **universal law of the seed** helps us to understand that concern, worry, and fear are seeds that produce thorns and choke out the Word of God. The moment we allow ourselves to become anxious, we're planting seeds in our heart that produce thorns and choke out what little confidence we do have in God. Jesus warned, *"But whoever does not have, even what he has will be taken away from him."*

In Philippians 4:4, Paul encourages us to, *"Rejoice in the Lord always. Again I will say, rejoice!"* **Rejoicing** is *a celebration of all the good things*. Rejoicing is usually the manifestation of a grateful person who notices all that's good. Searching for them, finding them, and celebrating them is a form of planting seeds in our heart that bloom into a bouquet full of all the reasons to trust God. The seed of God's truth emerges to ward off the seeds of fear and anxiety and is called the *shield of faith*!

Paul explains the mind-set of those who rejoice continually. By noticing the good things and expressing our thankfulness, we continuously affirm to our heart that God is our source of all that's good in our life. Proverbs 15:15 describes it this way, *"He who is of a merry heart has a continual feast."* The only way to ensure a merry heart is to continually ponder, think on, meditate, and acknowledge the good things in life. I like to say it this way, "Every day's a holiday, and every meal's a banquet!"

> *Finally, brethren, whatever things are true, whatever things are noble, whatever things are just, whatever things are pure, whatever things*

are lovely, whatever things are of good report, if there is any virtue and if there is anything praiseworthy — meditate on these things. The things which you learned and received and heard and saw in me, these do, and the God of peace will be with you. (Phil. 4:8)

This tranquility we have in God—this peace of mind—is based on the fact that we're in Jesus; therefore, all God's resources are available to us. We can't help but be at peace!

Yesterday, one of my incredible daughters, Summer, walked by my study a few times as I was recording. I knew she needed to talk after having just received a call from one of her sisters. My grandson had been in a sporting accident. The possibilities didn't look good. He had suffered a concussion and couldn't remember how old he was, what grade he was in, how many quarters were in a dollar, and his speech was slurred. The doctors feared brain trauma, broken facial bones, and ... well, you get the picture. Brenda, Summer, and I bowed and listened to the Lord for a few minutes, began to speak life over him, and then waited ... but for what, you might ask?

I have six daughters, fourteen grand-kids, and a great-grandchild. Believe me; we've gone through all the stuff that happens to kids. I've faced life-threatening illnesses, diseases, and injuries. Plus, I've traveled the world in dangerous situations where my life was threatened for preaching the gospel. When we face disaster, our first "knowing" is, "This isn't from God. God's not doing this. God's not sending this. God's not allowing this." From that place of peace, we always begin to speak life. Afterward, there's only one thing left to do: wait for peace to manifest, *"And let the peace of God rule (referee) in your hearts."* (Col. 3:15).

When peace comes, we know, no matter what, the outcome will be good. If peace doesn't come, something needs to be resolved in our heart. For this, we must always seek God's wisdom.

When we know and trust the God of Peace, Jehovah-Shalom, we experience *"The peace of God, which passes all understanding (defying circumstances and reason), guarding our hearts and minds."* Why? Because we know what is ours in Christ!

The Bible is chock-full of promises. Paul said, *"All the promises God ever made to anyone is yes for us, because we are in Jesus."* (2 Cor. 1:20) Do everything you can to renew your mind concerning His promises. As you daily meditate on them being yours, your heart will become established. When this happens, your first response to every negative or destructive situation will be a promise of God, which will bring peace and comfort.

If you're tired of getting "beat up" every Sunday; if you are ready to bathe you heart and mind in the Good News Jesus brought us about God, please visit: https://www.impactministries.com/welcome-to-impact-ministries/, to sign up for my free weekly video message. Disclaimer: this is only for believers who desire to live life at its best!

YOKE

A yoke can be something that restrains or shifts the burden off our shoulders. It all depends on who is leading!

Chapter 24

A PICTURE OF SATISFACTION AND CONTENTMENT

(Chaim Bentorah)

Matthew 11:28-30

> *Come unto me, all [ye] that labour and are heavy laden, and I will give you rest. Take my yoke upon you, and learn of me; for I am meek and lowly in heart: and ye shall find rest unto your souls. For my yoke [is] easy, and my burden is light.*

Many Christians live as if this passage of Scripture does not exist. They live in constant fear of committing some sin that will condemn them to hell. They live in fear that if they do not tithe ten percent of their gross income, or miss church one Sunday, or if they don't witness to others, or if they smoke, drink or break any number of rules, God will punish them. I am not saying we should cease to pursue good habits and take up bad ones; I am just saying we are not to follow them out of fear of an angry God who will strike us down if we break one rule.

We follow these rules as a way to express our love for God. Yet, there are so many Christians who follow rules and regulations out of fear. Does I John 4:18 not tell us that perfect love casts out all fear? Many of us are laboring and have become heavy-laden under the laws of God. Jesus is telling us that the law is not meant to be a burden, any more than the laws of marriage are to be a burden.

One law of marriage is that a husband does not cheat on his wife. He doesn't follow this law because he is afraid of an undesirable interface between his head and a frying pan. If he loves his wife, it will be the most natural thing for him not to lust after other women or cheat on his wife. She is meek and lowly in heart; her only desire is that she be the center of her husband's world, and if he loves her, she will be the center of his world.

Jesus is asking that we learn from Him, understanding that He is meek and lowly in heart and we will find rest.

The word in Greek for *rest* is *Ana Pauo*, which means to pause from labor. Jesus spoke this word in Aramaic, which is much more poetic and expressive. The Aramaic word for rest used in these passages is *Nucha*. It comes from an old Ugaritic word *NH* and the Akkadian and Persian word *Nahu*, which is a reference to a camel's resting place. Arabic grew out of the Persian language. There are about 160 words in Arabic for camel; this is one of them. When a Semitic person heard the word *Nucha*, he pictured a camel at rest, content, and satisfied. This is what a first-century Eastern man pictured when Jesus said that he would give him rest. He would give him a sense of satisfaction and contentment.

In the Western world we have little concept of what a camel is. We consider them unruly, temperamental, stubborn, and angry creatures. Actually, a camel is a docile and very sweet creature, under a caring hand. Only when it is ill-treated can it become stubborn and angry.

Although a camel can carry around 1,000 pounds, its master will burden him down with but just a third of that weight. In its origins as a pack animal, camels were used to carry frankincense, the fragrance of a king. Jesus is saying that He is the caring master, and the burden we carry is just the fragrance of our King, who does not force us to carry more than we can bear. When He gives us rest, he is like the camel driver, who allows his camels to relax and cool themselves. His burden is light, a burden yes, but one that carries His

> Although a camel can carry around 1,000 pounds, its master will not burden him down with but just a third of that weight.

fragrance does not break backs.

In Aramaic, Jesus is not saying that He is *meek* and *lowly* in heart, but that He is *restful, Nucha,* and *meek* in heart. He is our resting place. The ground is the resting place for a camel, but Jesus is our resting place. We lay in the arms of Jesus with all our burdens. As our resting place, he absorbs the weight of our burden.

Jesus also says that He is *meek in heart.* The word *meek* in Aramaic is *Makyaka, which* is to suck entirely out of; like sucking all the tea out of a paper cup with a straw. It carries the idea of all-consuming. Jesus is saying that His heart is consumed with us; we are the most important thing in the world to Him. His heart sucks us up entirely.

How can we even think that He means to overburden us? Just as a husband's heart is consumed with his wife's presence, such that she can rest in his arms as he shares whatever burden she may have. She knows that when she is wrapped in her husband's arms, her burden is his burden as well. When we wrap ourselves in the arms of God, our burden is His burden as well. As the husband shares his wife's burden, he will gently stroke her face with his fingers and say, "It's okay." And it suddenly becomes okay. Just as we find our *Nucha,* our *resting place* in the arms of God, He will gently stroke our face with His fingers and say, "It's okay." And suddenly, it is okay.

And like that camel on his *Nucha,* we become the picture of satisfaction and contentment.

To sign up for Chaim Bentorah's free daily Hebrew Word study, explore his books, and learn more about his in-depth biblical Hebrew online learning platform, please visit: https://www.chaimbentorah.com/

Chapter 25

HARMONIZING WITH GOD

To have God's strength, we simply keep in step with Him as He pulls the load!

According to Scripture, Jesus emptied Himself (Phil. 2:6-8) and became a real man with a human body (1 John 4:2-3), and was a man (Heb. 2:14-18) in every way as we are, yet without sin (Heb. 4:15). Besides the victories He won in His personal life, He operated in the gifts of the Holy Spirit throughout His ministry, working miracles, words of knowledge, and healing the sick.

Religion would have us believe He did all this because He was the Son of God, operating as God on Planet Earth. Jesus, however, explained that He cast out demons, healed the sick, and everything else He did because He was the Son of Man!

Jesus had to come to earth as a man for some fundamental reasons. God had given authority over Planet Earth to mankind. Jesus had to do all He did as a man filled with the Holy Spirit, or God would have violated His Word. In truth, the only reason it's legal for Jesus to come the second time to defeat the antichrist is because He'll defeat the man of iniquity as a man.

Another fundamental requisite for Jesus coming as a man was to model what a righteous man fully yielded to God would look like. Jesus Himself said, *"He who believes in Me, the works that I do he will do also; and greater works than these he will do, because I go to My Father."* (John 14:12)

These, like so many words of Jesus, have been explained away. Believers who dare to believe them are considered egomaniacs, delusional, or spiritually idealistic and counseled to give up their unrealistic faith in the words of Jesus! Once distrust in His teachings has sprouted, they settle into "a normal Christian life" devoid of power.

Jesus' words wouldn't seem so outlandish if we started with the essential truth: Jesus emptied Himself of all God-like power and became a man in every way, only without sin. The confidence we have is that His victory as a man means that we share in that victory. He's taught us His secret to a victorious personal life and a powerful ministry: being one with God!

> The church's refusal to believe the truth about the humanity of Jesus means He can never be our standard for human potentiality.

The church's refusal to believe the truth about the humanity of Jesus means He can never be our standard for human potentiality. The key to His words in John 14:12 are, *"He who believes on me."* He didn't say, "He who believes in His denominational version or personal idea of me." The implication is, *"He who believes on me"* as the Scripture says. A better way to understand it might be, "He who believes God's report about me!"

When challenged about His teachings, how He accomplished such seemingly phenomenal things (His source of power), and even His right to do those things, is patently defined. He performed the miraculous by the power of the Holy Spirit working through Him.

"God anointed Jesus of Nazareth with the Holy Spirit and with power, who went about doing good and healing all who were oppressed by the devil, for God was with Him." (Acts 10:38) He, like any other human being, relied on the power of God working through the Holy Spirit… the same Holy Spirit who lives in every believer.

Jesus continually reiterated that His teaching came straight from God's Word… the Scripture. The Jews of His day had the Torah for over 1,000 years. The problem was, they had interpreted it by the Talmud and oral traditions for so many years that they didn't seem to recognize it when they heard it. Maybe it was because they, like modern Christians, knew the religious interpretation but not the Word itself.

Do you not believe that I am in the Father, and the Father in Me? The words that I speak to you I do not speak on My own authority, but the Father who dwells in Me does the works. Believe Me that I am in the Father and the Father in Me, or else believe Me for the sake of the works themselves. (John 14:10-11)

Where this becomes the most challenging for us is when Jesus explains why He has authority—the right to work miracles, heal the sick, and cast out demons: *"For as the Father… has given Him authority to execute judgment also, because He is the Son of Man."* (John 5:26-27) Every time He uses the phrase *"Son of Man,"* Jesus is informing us that He's doing what can only be done on Planet Earth by a man; otherwise, it would be a violation of God's Word!

All of these factors… in fact, everything Jesus did to represent God on Planet Earth can be understood in one word: *harmony!* Jesus emptied Himself of His power as God, becoming a man in every way to demonstrate how we can manifest and express the power of God! As a full-blooded man, He's our example in every way! He won every personal and ministerial battle utilizing the same power and process available to us all, and He explained how we could do the same.

Jesus' "big secret" is this, *"I and My Father are one."* (John 10:30) Jesus never did anything that wasn't based on the Scripture—the Word and intention of the Father. He surrendered His every personal opinion to God's opinion as expressed in the Scripture. Every miracle, every healing was congruent with God's name and God's Word. He harmonized every aspect of His life with the revealed knowledge of God.

Jesus never introduced anything new about God. Even the Covenant that was established through His resurrection had already been revealed in the Old Testament. What Jesus did do, however, was represent God's Words from God's original intention: to love mankind and provide the best life possible. The religious community didn't hate Him because He improperly represented God; they hated Him because His representation of God revealed their carnal, corrupt, power-driven misrepresentation of God! They were going to lose control of the people!

Jesus exposed the religious leaders' power-hungry attempt to take the Kingdom by force in one compelling statement found in Matthew 11:12. Sadly, even Christians lift this statement out of context and extol force as a virtue, but the Kingdom can't be taken by force. The NKJV says, "*The kingdom of heaven suffers violence.*" Wuest translates it as, "*The kingdom of heaven is being taken by storm, and the strong and forceful ones claim it for themselves.*" And, finally, the Amplified's (AMP) rendering, "*The Kingdom of heaven has suffered assault, and violent men seize it by force [as a precious prize — a share in the heavenly kingdom is sought with most ardent zeal and intense exertion].*"

Jesus juxtaposes those who attempt to use force with those who follow His example. He harmonized with the Father. He didn't try to force anything, choosing instead to humble Himself and flow with God, based on the Scripture, in every situation. Then, He offered us this same life, free from force, by yoking up with Him: harmonizing!

Western Christianity is a culture of force and violence. Catholicism, Martin Luther, and other reformists killed and tortured those who disagreed with their doctrine. Jesus never used violence or force to bring someone into the kingdom; He always displayed the goodness of God to bring men to repentance (Rom. 2:4).

In some circles, over the last 50 years, there's been a renewed interest in the "in Christ" realities. Most of those who present this incredible doctrine do so from a legalistic or positional perspective. Once a doctrine moves away from the realm of faith and life application, it becomes meaningless and powerless, even if the teaching is technically correct. In the absence of personal faith (trust and intention), it's erroneously believed truth should automatically happen, i.e., all the benefits of being "in Christ" should magically appear apart from our choice, trust, desire, or intention! If this were true, no one would need faith, and the world would be a wonderful place!

The yoke represents, among other things, the concept of harmony. When two oxen are yoked together, they pair a leader (Jesus) with a follower (the believer). For this pairing to work, the follower must keep in step with the leader. Galatians 5:16 tells us to, "*Walk in the Spirit, and you shall not fulfill the lust of the flesh.*" In other words, there must be a desire and intention on our part.

Verse 25 reiterates the importance that, "*If we live in the Spirit, let us also walk in the Spirit.*" Once again, we see the concept of harmonizing by keeping in step. Living or being in the Spirit is of no benefit if we don't walk in the Spirit or keep in step. If we don't harmonize with the Spirit, we will walk in the flesh which, according to Romans 8:13, kills us!

Several core factors hinder us from harmonizing with God. First and foremost is ignorance of the Scripture. Our ignorance of the Scripture isolates us from the reality that everything Jesus said was what God had already said. He was in harmony with God. Every miracle He performed was based on the names of God. He was in harmony with God's testimony of Himself! Even the Scripture Jesus presented as the cornerstone for interpretation and application of all truth was exactly as God had said from the beginning, *"Love the Lord your God... love your neighbor as yourself."* (Matt. 22:37-39) He wasn't presenting a new image of God; it was the same word heard from the beginning.

> *I write no new commandment to you, but an old commandment which you have had from the beginning. The old commandment is the word which you heard from the beginning. Again, a new commandment I write to you, which thing is true in Him and in you, because the darkness is passing away, and the true light is already shining.* (1 John 2:7-8)

The only thing new about this commandment is that it's made new in Christ. Because of His representation of God, the darkness passing so we can finally see God as He is.

As Chaim Bentorah so eloquently points out, the word **good** in the Hebrew means *pleasing and desirable*, and it always has the concept of harmony. In other words, what makes anything desirable, pleasant, and lifegiving is the fact that it's not only in harmony with God, but it draws us personally into harmony with God. It's not simply a legal position; it's a lifestyle based on core beliefs and a way of treating others that's in perfect harmony with all God has ever done and all He will ever do.

In the same chapter that tells us of Jesus emptying Himself, Paul tells us how to move into that harmony with God where we live as He lived, minister as He ministered, and treat others the way He treated them, *"Let this mind be in you which was also in Christ Jesus."* (Phil 2:5) It all starts with emptying ourselves of all that's not in harmony with God as Jesus represented Him.

Jesus became a man just like us, with all our limitations, yet without sin. When we were born again, we were made righteous just like him, having been cleansed from all sin. He yielded to the Holy Spirit, just as we too can yield to the Holy Spirit. He never taught or believed anything in conflict with the Scriptures or the names of God. Harmonizing His beliefs with God's was a way of life, just as ours should be... if we want the same quality of life He has!

You may want to do one of my favorite Heart exercises. After reading John 14:12, I immediately read a story about Jesus healing the sick or working a miracle. I, then, close my eyes and imagine it was me in that same situation ministering to the person in need. I pay close attention to every thought, every reaction, and every resistance that emerges. Then, I acknowledge, "Jesus, you're my Lord; I'm in you and you said I could do everything you did. Lead me into this kind of life and ministry."

Is there an area of your life where you keep fighting the same battle over and over? Maybe things start going well in this area, but you know once it reaches a certain point it's all going to collapse again. This is an indication of what the Bible would identify as a heart boundary. Proverbs teaches that all limitations come not from an outside attack, but from the limiting beliefs of our own heart.

Jesus taught us the one and only way to overcome negative, self-destructive heart beliefs. But what He taught is completely rejected by traditional religion, even though it is plainly laid out in the Gospels. If you are ready to put an end to these repetitious destructive cycles I want to put one of the most powerful books you'll ever read into your hands; *Moving Your Invisible Boundaries*. If you've circled that mountain for the last time, this will give you the information, the tools and the know how to change the beliefs of your heart and expand your boundaries. Please visit: https://www.impactministries.com/product/moving-your-invisible-boundaries-book/ to check out *Moving Your Invisible Boundaries*.

WHAT NOW?

Knowing what to do is a torment until we do it!

Chapter 26

WHAT NOW?

The man driven by ego is content to know; the man hungry for life makes it work!

The Apostle Peter presented the truth of the end of this world and the beginning of a new world. Then, he asked the question we should ask every time we read a truth in the Word of God, "In light of this, '*what manner of persons ought [I] to be in holy conduct and godliness.*" (2 Pet. 3:11-13)

For nearly half a century, I've preached, taught, encouraged, advised, and counseled people who were seeking answers based on God's Word. I've observed consistent patterns of behavior, as well as similar questions and comments from those who never seem to find abundant life. The majority tended to bemoan, "If only we had an operating manual for how life works!" When it was pointed out that there was a manual, AKA *The Bible*, they usually responded with, "But it's so hard to understand."

I experience two frustrations when hearing these types of statements. First, I do realize religion has made God's Word confusing, contradictory, and hard to understand. I also realize, however, that those who open their heart to rely on the Holy Spirit as their teacher and read God's Word themselves will always come to the knowledge of the truth.

This, of course, leads to my second frustration, "Why aren't you reading this for yourself?" The answer is usually, "I'm afraid I won't get it right." Jesus once told a parable about talents. The man who received one talent

What Now?

did nothing it. Because he judged the master to be ruthless and unjust, he buried his talent in the ground. The scripture reveals his real issue to be wickedness and laziness (Matt. 25:26). His judgment against God became the seed He planted, and the fruit it produced was exactly as he expected.

Paul tells us to *"Work out our own salvation."* (Phil. 2:12) Our eternal well-being, as well as the quality of our life here on earth, is a matter of salvation! We can't be so slothful, lackadaisical, and irresponsible that we allow someone else to hear from and define God for us, as the children of Israel requested of Moses. The only reason we'd hand such an awesome responsibility to someone else is unbelief. At the end of the day, we must ask ourselves appropriate questions and choose our course of action.

When we attend a church service, everything the preacher said is consummated in an altar call that requires a decision. Every altar call comes down to this one question, "In light of what I now know, what decisions will I make about how to live and manage my life?" Likewise, after reading this book, what will you do differently?

1. Will I stop improperly interpreting the words that make me perceive God in a negative light?
2. Will I ALWAYS qualify everything I hear, read, and think by what Jesus taught, modeled, and accomplished through the death, burial, and resurrection?
3. Will I continue to listen to those who present God as angry and vengeful?
4. Will I seek new ways to interact with God through Bible reading, study, and prayer?
5. Will I repent of blaming God for the hardships, tests, and trials in my life?
6. Will I accept that my every decision has consequences and that I'm living out the consequences of those decisions?
7. Will I seek to put God's Word into application in my life?
8. Will I define love based solely on God's commandments?
9. Will I trust God and turn to Him for wisdom and guidance in my every decision?
10. Will I seek to be a doer and not just a hearer of His Word?

Jesus provides us with incredible insight into how we can move from information into experiential knowledge by one simple shift of intention. Faith is always associated with intention. The Hebrew word for *said* in the scripture, *"And God said, 'Let there be light,"* doesn't emphasize the fact that He spoke but that He first conceived every aspect of it in His heart with intention. He intended for His spoken Word to produce exactly what He saw in His heart![15]

Faith is activated into **great faith** when there's an intention to act. Without the intention to act or apply it, we have **dead faith** (James 2:20). Because Abraham believed in the promise God had made to him, he took his family from Ur of Chaldees to the land to which God had called him. When Moses believed God, he set out to Egypt to challenge Pharaoh and set the people free. All the believers listed in the Hebrews 11 roll call of faith were people who listened and believed intending to take action.

Jesus made this clear when He said, *"My doctrine is not mine but His who sent me."* (John 7:16) We never experientially know if what we believe is true or not until it works. When it works just as the Word promises, we become sure, confident, and immovable. Hearers of the Word don't trust God enough to run any personal risk. They're always listening and waiting to see if it will happen on its own. Since they seldom, if ever, attempt to put anything into practice, they never experience the life and power of God. As a result, the more they learn, the more unbelieving and discouraged they become.

Jesus went on to say, *"If anyone wills to do His will, he shall know concerning the doctrine, whether it is from God or whether I speak on My own authority."* (John 7:17) The first word for *wills* has to do with *determination, resolve, has the purpose, takes delight*, i.e., the intention to do, apply, or practice. Only in the application of truth will we discover if the doctrine being preached is true.

You'll never know if one word of this book is true until you determine to put it into practice. No one can tell you precisely what that will look like in your life. Only you know the places this truth has challenged you. Only

---

15   To say, to answer, to say in one's heart, to think, to command, to promise, to intend

From The Online Bible Thayer's Greek Lexicon and Brown Driver & Briggs Hebrew Lexicon, Copyright © 1993, Woodside Bible Fellowship, Ontario, Canada. Licensed from the Institute for Creation Research.

you know the way religion has influenced your thinking in the past. Others can make suggestions, but only you know, "Unless I use this truth to overcome _____, I'll never be the person I want to be!"

The moment you determine to believe the truth, commit to putting it into practice, and acknowledge your dependence on God for strength, you'll begin to grow in grace—God's freely-given power, strength, and ability. Take the plunge! Make the decision! Experience His grace!

Romans 5:2, "*We have access by faith into this grace in which we stand, and rejoice in the hope of the glory of God.*"

If you want access to hundreds of free videos and other teachings that focus on God as He presented Himself through His name, His Word and the Lord Jesus Christ, join me every week for *Dr. Jim Richards' Life at its best!*

About Dr. Jim Richards

In 1972, Dr. James B. Richards accepted Christ and answered the call to ministry. His dramatic conversion and passion for helping hurting people launched him onto the streets of Huntsville, Alabama. Early on in his mission to reach teenagers and drug abusers, his ministry quickly grew into a home church that eventually led to the birth of Impact Ministries.

Before his salvation, Jim was a professional musician with all the trappings of a worldly lifestyle. More than anything, he was searching for true freedom. Sick of himself and his empty pursuits, he hated all that his life had become. He turned to drugs as a means of escape and relief. Although he was desperate to find God, his emotional outrage made people afraid to tell him about Jesus. As he searched for help, he only became more confused and hopeless than ever.

After listening to his bass player grumbling about a verse of Scripture that a Christian had shared with him, Jim had a miraculous encounter with God. From this one Scripture, he was able to experience God's love! He gave his life to the Lord and was set free from his addictions. His whole life changed! Now, after years of ministry, Jim still believes there is no one that God cannot help, and there is no one God does not love. He has committed his life to help people experience that love. If his life is a model for anything, it is that God never quits on anyone.

With doctorates in theology, human behavior and alternative medicine, and an honorary doctorate in world evangelism, Jim has received certified training as a detox specialist and drug counselor. His uncompromising, yet positive, approach to the gospel strengthens, instructs and challenges people to new levels of victory, power, and service. Jim's extensive experience in working with substance abuse, codependency, and other social/emotional issues has led him to pioneer effective, creative, Bible-based approaches to ministry that meet the needs of today's world.

Most importantly, Jim believes that people need to be made whole by experiencing God's unconditional love. His messages are simple, practical, and powerful. His passion is to change the way the world sees God so that people can experience a relationship with Him through Jesus.

Jim and his wife, Brenda, have six daughters, 14 grandchildren, and a great-grandchild. They continue to reside in Huntsville, Alabama.

For additional content and resources, please visit: https://www.impact-ministries.com/

About Chaim Bentorah

"Chaim Bentorah" is the pseudonym of a Gentile Christian who taught college-level Biblical Hebrew and is an Amazon Bestselling Author.

He prepared his students to take the placement exams for graduate school. He has now developed a method of study where he can prepare any believer, regardless of age or academic background, to study the Word of God using Biblical Hebrew.

Chaim Bentorah received his B.A. degree from Moody Bible Institute in Jewish Studies and his M.A. degree from Denver Seminary in Old Testament and Hebrew and his PhD in Biblical Archeology. His Doctoral Dissertation was on the "Esoteric Structure of the Hebrew Alphabet." He has taught Classical Hebrew at World Harvest Bible College for thirteen years and also taught Hebrew for three years as a language course for Christian Center High School.

He presently sends out a Hebrew word study to thousands of subscribers each day and hosts the in-depth biblical Hebrew learning platform at https://www.hebrewwordstudy.com/. To subscribe to Chaim Bentorah's free daily word study, learn more about his books and his in-depth Hebrew Learning platform, please visit:https://www.chaimbentorah.com/.

www.ingramcontent.com/pod-product-compliance
Lightning Source LLC
Chambersburg PA
CBHW071910110426
R18126600001B/R181266PG42743CBX00012B/5